A DAY IN A DALE

Yvette Huddleston
Walter Swan

A DAY IN A DALE

To Vivian and John.

with best wishes

Yvette Huddleston

Walter Swan

Scratching Shed Publishing Ltd

First published by Scratching Shed Publishing Ltd in 2011
Registered in England & Wales No. 6588772.
Registered office:
47 Street Lane, Leeds, West Yorkshire. LS8 1AP

www.scratchingshedpublishing.co.uk

ISBN 978-0956478740

Unless stated otherwise, all photographs are by Walter Swan

A catalogue record for this book is available from the British Library.

Typeset in Warnock Pro Semi Bold and Palatino

Printed and bound in the United Kingdom by
L.P.P.S.Ltd, Wellingborough, Northants, NN8 3PJ

Contents

Note on recommended maps: Ordnance Survey maps covering the Yorkshire Dales National Park are EX030 Yorkshire Dales North and Central and EX002 Yorkshire Dales South and West. These are best for detail and for walking. For more general information try the Landranger OS Maps LR099 Northallerton and Ripon, Pateley Bridge and Leyburn and LR092 Barnard Castle and Richmond. The Yorkshire Tourist Board also provides an official tourist map of Yorkshire which is useful for route planning.

ACKNOWLEDGEMENTS

We would like to thank everyone we met during our days in the dales for their helpfulness, friendliness, humour and warmth – and for their generosity in sharing their stories with us

THE AUTHORS

Yvette Huddleston has been a freelance journalist for twenty-one years. She was a film columnist for the *Daily Mail* for ten years and has contributed features and reviews to a variety of national and regional publications including the *Daily Telegraph, Empire Film Magazine* and the *Yorkshire Post*. After living in London for many years, she moved to Ilkley with her family eleven years ago.

Walter Swan is a freelance writer who has also enjoyed a career in English teaching and broadcasting – he has worked as a researcher and programme associate for the BBC, LWT and Sky. With Yvette he has been a regular contributor to the *Yorkshire Post* and *Yorkshire Ridings Magazine*. A keen amateur photographer, he has lived in Burley-in-Wharfedale since 1997.

Scaleber Force,
near Settle

INTRODUCTION

The chapters that follow represent diaries of over two dozen excursions, each lasting a day, into the Yorkshire Dales – God's own country. On every occasion, we drove to our chosen dale but regularly made use of our walking boots to explore further afield. Our purpose was to see what we could see, who we might meet, and report on our day out for features which have been appearing over a period of five years in the *Yorkshire Post Magazine*. We quickly discovered that a vital element in capturing the essence of any dale was to meet the people who live, work or holiday there and allow their words to add further colour to our own experiences.

We have chosen to present the updated and expanded versions of our original articles in geographical rather than chronological order. The first dale we visited for the *Yorkshire Post* series of features was Coverdale as, at that time, our intention was to bring readers' attention to the lesser known dales, and this was certainly one of the least travelled. Since then, our project has expanded to include favourite stretches of the better known dales – Swaledale, Wensleydale and Wharfedale – as well as hidden gems like Raydale and Cotter Dale.

We cannot pretend that this is an exhaustive exploration of every dale there is to be found in the Yorkshire Dales National Park: rather,

Welcome to the Dales

we provide examples of the kind of day you yourself might experience if you are day-tripping using a car. Of course, this book can also be used as a guide by those who are basing themselves in the Dales for longer than a day at a time, much the best way of seeing the glories of this most beautiful part of Yorkshire, if the opportunity permits.

Every chapter is rounded off with a fact file of useful contacts and information for tourists and holiday-makers, particularly those seeking out local hostelries and bed and breakfast accommodation.

Our wish is that in following in our footsteps, or tyre tracks, you enjoy your day in a dale on every occasion just as much as we did, and will continue to do with our constant re-visits.

Yvette Huddleston and Walter Swan

THE WESTERN DALES

Kingsdale, Deepdale, Dentdale, Widdale,
Chapel le Dale, Ribblesdale, Malhamdale

A panoramic
view of
Deepdale

THE PARADISE DALES
Kingsdale and Deepdale (July)

Many people, in their rush to the Lakes, drive through a small portion of Ingleton on the A65 without appreciating how much more of the town there is to see. Ingleton is famed for its waterfalls walk, which is where knowledgeable visitors head for, but the old part of the town, close to the church, is also well worth visiting. St Mary's stands on the site of the original Norman church – it still has a thirteenth century tower – and its picturesque setting on a hill overlooking Twiss Beck affords delightful views down to the river and the impressive railway viaduct.

Ingleton, which stands at the point where the Rivers Twiss and Doe converge to become the Greta, makes much of its living from water – there's even an outdoor heated swimming pool, a classic art deco design, well known in the area and open between May and September. It was built in 1933 by a small but enthusiastic group of local volunteers; their task was made easier by the fact that just as the first sods of turf were being dug, miners at the local colliery went on strike and offered their labouring services in digging out the pool.

We arrived in Ingleton en route to Kingsdale, but stopped to make some purchases at the Ingleton Pottery and enjoy the entertainment and wit of the remarkable Dick Unsworth who unselfconsciously

The clouds gather over Kingsdale

declares himself to be the only one-handed potter in the country. Dick runs the business, which was established in 1971, with his wife Jill and son Dan – all three are potters, though Dick quipped that 'their stuff isn't a patch on mine.' His sense of humour as he led us through the process of hand throwing the pots (he was planning to make seventy-five mugs on the day of our visit), his knowledge about all things connected with the making and firing of pots and his consummate skill as an artist helped half an hour to pass by extremely entertainingly.

The Unsworth family make and sell everything from jugs, mugs and bowls to wine goblets, vases, carafes and tea-light holders – and all are very reasonably priced. We were also tempted into taking some refreshment at the Curlew Café and Craft Centre, a welcoming place with friendly staff and packed full of gifts, pictures and photographs of the local area. The lady who served us told us about the Forties event that the village had hosted the previous weekend. 'Everyone was dressed up in uniform and we had a Spitfire fly by,' she enthused. 'It was great fun for everyone. We held the first one last year but we're hoping it will continue.'

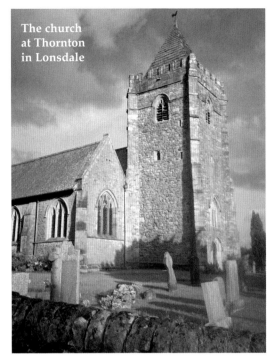

The church at Thornton in Lonsdale

Thornton Force

The view from Thornton in Lonsdale

While we were having our coffee, and a tasty homemade cherry scone, a Derbyshire couple on a neighbouring table enquired whether the walking stick they had accidentally left behind at the café on a trip to Ingleton some months previously had been found. They were delighted when the lady fetched it out from the back of the shop, saying, 'I kept it specially, thinking you might come back for it.'

During a quick walk around the town, we saw Pearson's, the award-winning butcher's and delicatessen shop, several outdoor clothing stores, an intriguing shop called Elemental selling Fair Trade goods, and an inviting-looking Italian restaurant called La Tavernetta. We also tried to look in on the church, which is quite a size for a relatively small community, but unfortunately it was closed. In front of the church, the First World War memorial listed forty-one dead, a huge number of young men considering the overall population of Ingleton.

Many of the dales towns and villages we have visited during our excursions have an Olde Sweete Shoppe and Ingleton was no exception. It's always a pleasure to browse through the appealing merchandise in these tempting places and wallow in sweetie nostalgia, so we popped in and bought some old-fashioned and much needed cough sweets, such was the summer we were having.

From Ingleton we took the Yorkshire Dales Cycleway by following signs to the Waterfalls Walk. The walk is an unmissable and utterly delightful four and a half mile route through lovely glades of ancient oak woodland and open moorland during which time the visitor comes across a series of breathtaking waterfalls and spectacular geological features. The most famous and impressive of the waterfalls (located a mile and a half from the car park) is the mighty Thornton Force with its huge pool and tumbling cascade as the river plunges fourteen metres over limestone rocks. We'd say more, but if you only have a day in a dale, you might need to set aside a significant portion of a morning or afternoon to doing justice to the Waterfalls Walk. One further word of advice: wait for a wet spell to ensure seeing the falls at their most dramatic, but visit on a dry day!

Next, we followed the B road out to Thornton in Lonsdale – don't miss the turning off on the right or you'll find yourself back on the A65. Sadly, the church of St Oswald's is only open on Mondays between two and four in the afternoon, so we didn't see the interior – but it certainly looks very impressive from the outside. It's a sign of the times that the need is felt to keep the church locked when there is no-one there to supervise. Opposite the church was the Marston Arms Hotel which, according to a sign above the door, dates back well over three centuries to 1679. We would love to have called in but we'd lunched already and our day was all too swiftly passing with the journey into Kingsdale barely begun.

At the church you turn right and continue steadily upwards. Before long we came upon Thornton Hall, a grandly rugged-looking building, now obviously a farmhouse. In a different setting, (in other words, on an exposed moor) Thornton Hall could easily be Wuthering Heights. We would have had wonderful views over to Ingleborough (ignoring the car park at White Scar Cave and the Ingleton granite quarry) if only the weather had been kinder and less dismal. That's why it's worth returning more than once (as we have subsequently done), to see what you've missed when the clouds keep as low as they so often do. You continue climbing the hill, then descend again briefly, then climb once more before coming to the remarkable straight section of Kingsdale

Deepdale Waterfall

Beck – it might almost be a canal – before it feeds southwards into the River Twiss and its various afore-mentioned waterfalls.

We stopped at the little footbridge looking north towards another of the Three Peaks, Whernside, and tried to capture the potentially splendid photographic image of the footbridge and the beck with Whernside looming in the distance. We succeeded in getting some promising shots – and then disaster struck. The camera somehow toppled out of the bag it was in and plunged straight into the beck. It's no mere pun to say there was a terrible sinking feeling. Almost all of the pictures taken for the Day in a Dale series for the previous two years had been taken with this camera, now wedged between rocks some two feet under the water. Some cameras are waterproof but, sadly, not this one. We retrieved it, but the damage was done: this was an ex-camera. The consequence was that we were obliged to use a considerably inferior digital camera for the remainder of the trip, uncertain as to whether the memory card still inside the old one had survived the sudden submergence.

Inevitably, every view we saw from that moment onwards cried out to be snapped by a far better camera than the one we were now using.

A Day In A Dale

An ideal crossing point in Kingsdale

Even so, it is the memory of the day and the immediacy and impact of the moment which matters more than any photographic image, images that will remain indelibly. At least, that is how we tried to console ourselves.

The next landmark was Kingsdale Head, where self-catering accommodation is available. Despite there being no other properties in sight for miles around, it's comforting to know that Ingleton and Dent are no great distance away for anyone holidaying in a location perfect

21

for leaving the hustle and bustle of modern life far behind. It's here that you come across the first of several gates across the road as you continue towards Deepdale, a vital means of keeping local livestock from straying too far. Try to arrange to have a willing passenger to do the opening and closing – or keep your patience if you are on your own.

What is remarkable about the road through Kingsdale is that for much of the way you are extremely close to Whernside, affording quite awe-inspiring views of the gentle looking mountain. What was also apparent, though, was that there appear to be no designated paths for walkers up to the summit from this side of the peak, though there was a signpost for a footpath to nearby Barbondale. This is very definitely caving country with treacherous shake holes, caves and potholes dotting the landscape. The road never crosses the watercourse but there are occasional little bridges where tributaries burble down the valley side and feed into the Kingsdale Beck.

There are only isolated pockets of civilisation, as you continue driving, in the form of an occasional farm or barn. In time you cease climbing up the winding lane, and crest the brow of a hill. You are now greeted with a most amazing, overwhelming view down into Deepdale. The clouds, by this time, had lifted, and with it our mood, despite the loss of the camera. We agreed that this was possibly the most beautiful view we had seen in all our dales travels, an opinion we continue to share. To come across such a perfect vista – and unexpectedly, too, for the first-time visitor – really takes the breath away: that view alone is worth travelling a long way for. A little further down the hill was another wonderful surprise when we 'discovered' an idyllic little glade on the roadside with a picture-perfect waterfall.

Once you drop down into Deepdale itself there is again remarkably little sign of human life – you come across one or two houses but they are very much alone with no near neighbours, apart from the occasional farm. However, unlike higher up, there were now more frequent signposts indicating routes for walkers. After a T junction we turned to the left, then followed a winding route into Dent – and if you have never been here, take our word, you have missed an absolute delight. It is a quite enchanting oasis of a village, parts of which seem to belong to a former century. You drive over narrow cobbled streets bordered by low stone houses, each one with its own character and attractive in a slightly different way. Winding little cobbled lanes lead off in various directions inviting you to explore and take your time. With more time, and with a proper replacement camera in hand, we felt we were certain to return to do Dent proper justice – and we have on several occasions since!

A FOOTNOTE. Once we'd got the camera home, there was just enough life in it to try linking it up to the computer to attempt to download the images. Remarkably, all the pictures we had taken had survived. However, once the download was completed, the camera finally gave up the ghost. It seemed like an heroic effort on the part of an inanimate object, retaining just enough life to give us a treasured visual record of a hugely enjoyable day not in one but in two dales.

Fact File

Kingsdale Head Cottage
(self catering), Westhouse, Ingleton, LA6 3PH.
☎ 015242 41393

Ingleton Pottery
Ingleton, North Yorks LA6 3HB
☎ 01524 241363;
⌨ www.ingletonpottery.co.uk
Workshop tours and demonstrations are available for groups by appointment.

Ingleton Waterfalls Walk
☎ 015242 41930
⌨ www.ingletonwaterfallswalk.co.uk

Ingleton Open Air Heated Swimming Pool
☎ 015242 41147
Open May to September
⌨ www.ingletonpool.co.uk

Curlew Café
Main Street, Ingleton LA6 3HQ,
☎ 01524 241608
⌨ www.curlewcrafts.com

White Scar Cave
Ingleton, North Yorkshire, LA6 3AW,
☎ 01524 241244.
⌨ www.whitescarcave.co.uk

Arten Gill
viaduct in
Dentdale

THE SECRET DALE
Dentdale (June)

If it is true that Dentdale is sometimes called The Secret Dale, it is only a secret in that those who know about its outstanding beauty are trying to keep it to themselves – and once you've discovered it, it's not difficult to understand why. The passage of time does not seem to have taken its toll on this dale: it permits a modern means of living, with farming being its predominant activity, while preserving a powerful sense of the best of the past.

If you are not arriving here via Kingsdale and Deepdale (described to us as 'Paradise' by one local), an excellent way of appreciating Dentdale is to come from the east via Newby Head Gate (on the road between the Ribblehead Viaduct and Hawes). There is no literal gate, but this is the gateway into the upper reaches of Dentdale where much of this section of a quiet, tranquil road doubles up as the Ribble Way and Dales Way, so do pay proper attention to the safety of walkers. Cyclists also make good use of this section of road, and small wonder – it must be one of the most beautiful designated routes anywhere in the country.

It won't be long before your eye is drawn to Dent Head viaduct, part of the Settle-Carlisle line and therefore in regular use. Built at much the same time as the world-famous Ribblehead Viaduct (in this case between 1870 and 1875) what distinguishes Dent Head is that it was built from blue limestone. The nearer you get to it, the more beautiful it seems – and then you find that the road passes right next to it. As Fell End Gill passes under a road bridge, there's a parking area to your right, with attractive falls and an ancient packbridge in clear view. Sheep had claimed the bridge as their own the day we visited, two of them quite blatantly posing when we produced the camera. What you'll really want to take pictures of, though, are the towering arches of the viaduct which seem to stride majestically overhead, dwarfing the trees.

But that's not the end of the man-made wonders which mingle with the beauty of the natural landscape. Follow the road a little further, alongside the watercourse's regular delightful falls (on its way towards becoming the River Dee), and you come to yet another viaduct at Arten Gill – in fact the highest viaduct on the Settle-Carlisle line. With eleven arches, a length of two hundred and twenty yards and a height of one hundred and seventeen feet, it is a truly imposing sight as its dominates the ravine of the Artengill Beck en route northwards to England's highest mainline station, Dent Station (actually some little distance from Dent itself).

You have to turn off the road to get the best view of the viaduct, and it's advisable to explore the area around the beck on foot. An information board helpfully explains the industrial history of the locality, paying special attention to the renovation that has taken place to restore dry-stone walls, fords, gateways and kilns in the vicinity. The kilns, some of which date back at least one hundred and fifty years, were used to produce quicklime. This corrosive compound was frequently used in the past, rather surprisingly one might think, to help make plaster and mortar and, when spread on the fields, to 'sweeten' the grass.

There's arguably no sweeter way to spend time than visiting a traditional Dales pub so calling in at The Sportsman's Inn at Cowgill (which also offers very reasonably priced bed and breakfast accommodation) will add to your day out. This photogenic, three hundred-year-old Grade II listed building is proud to proclaim that it is 'not a restaurant that sells beer, we are a seventeenth century inn that provides quality food and ales at a reasonable price.' It's a pub that

**Lucy Sandys-Clarke
the Dentdale blacksmith**

makes no concessions to modern trends, so you won't find a jukebox or Sky Sports – and there's no point in pulling out your mobile phone because they are not welcomed and you wouldn't get a signal anyway. The only signals are on the nearby railway line – so, if you can't get to the area by any other means, take a train.

A Day In A Dale

An ancient packbridge
at Dent Head viaduct

Dentdale

Hence our next stop was Dent Station. On the Settle to Carlisle line, it is, at one thousand one hundred and fifty feet above sea level, the highest railway station in England. The station house, built in 1885 and a Grade II listed property, is now a well appointed holiday home. It has been sympathetically renovated retaining many original features, including signs for the waiting room and porters, and is tastefully decorated with railway memorabilia such as a stationmaster's hat, lanterns and old travel posters.

From the elevated position at the station, you can enjoy breathtaking long distance views westwards towards Whernside and to the village of Dent which gives the dale its name. Heading down towards Dent, we stopped off in the small outlying village of Cowgill to visit the church of St John's, a lovely simple-looking church with long narrow windows, its only ornamentation being a small porch and bell turret. Built in 1838 on the site of an old chapel, it's in a beautiful location, close to a narrow, eighteenth century road bridge over the River Dee. Walking back to the car, we met local farmer Johnny Akrigg who runs Yewgales camping and caravan site where, for a small fee, you can also park for the day if you plan to walk in the area. 'I've

29

lived on the farm for over sixty-seven years,' says Johnny. 'My granddad and my mum and dad were here before me. I have been abroad – I'm just back from two months holiday in Lanzarote – but I prefer it here in Dentdale.' The campsite is a successful piece of diversification. 'We get a lot of people camping here in July,' he says, 'and there's one lady who comes up from Bristol every year; she's in her nineties now.'

Driving on along the narrow lane from Cowgill, beyond the dry stone walls on either side were sunny meadows of wildflowers – the yellow of the buttercups and rich russet of sheep's sorrel, punctuated by the odd poppy here and there, combining to create a spellbinding vista.

On the outskirts of Dent, we met up with Jim and Doreen Bolton. They moved to their idyllic-looking old farmhouse, which dates back to at least 1506 and is a listed building, from Blackpool more than twenty years ago. 'We always used to come to the Dales on holiday – never been anywhere else,' says Jim, 'and then we bought this place. It needed a lot of work doing on it. We did two years of coming up at weekends and holidays to work on it and then we just thought: "Why don't we just move up here?"'

'So we bit the bullet,' says Doreen. 'Jim came up here alone to start with and then I moved up a little later.' Both found work at one of the biggest local employers, Lyon Equipment, a distributor of outdoor leisure equipment. Opposite the house they now live in was a derelict outbuilding which had been scheduled for demolition in 1984 but Jim and Doreen brought it back from the brink and it is now a three star rated holiday cottage open all year round. It has proved to be very successful. 'We get lots of repeat bookings and word of mouth recommendations,' says Doreen. The couple love living in Dentdale. 'Everyone has always been very welcoming,' says Jim, 'from the moment we got here. Commuting to work was great; you'd meet three cars on the journey – and that was on a busy day!' Doreen says that they have always felt part of the community: 'Our nearest neighbours are a farming family who have been here for generations and they are the best neighbours you could have. Living here,' she adds, 'we count our blessings every day.'

The village of Dent, a cobble-stoned, narrow-laned historical

View across Dentdale

delight, is officially in Cumbria but also part of the Yorkshire Dales National Park and in the past was known as Dent Town. Dentdale celebrates its past with pride and a perfect example of this is the Dent Village Heritage Centre, set up in 2006 on the site of the old village petrol station by Jim and Margaret Taylor from High Laning Farm. Their granddaughter, Michelle Bentham, who was selling tickets on the door when we visited, explained how this remarkable museum came about. 'My grandparents have been collecting lots of artefacts and machinery for about the past thirty years – and it's all in here now!'

Through their extensive collection, the past is kept alive. A series of exhibitions illustrate the variety of means by which the people of Dentdale in years gone by endeavoured to extract a living from a countryside which seems idyllic to the passing tourist but which could be cruel and pitiless to those dependent on it for their livelihood. You could spend several hours looking around the Heritage Centre as it is packed full of interesting historical information, items and anecdotes.

We learned about the Sill family, wealthy eighteenth century Liverpool slave traders who kept African slaves on their estate at

Whernside Manor; Dent's most famous son, renowned geologist Adam Sedgwick, whose stone memorial stands in the centre of the village; and the 'terrible knitters'. The adjective, one quickly appreciates, is not a comment on the quality of goods – socks, caps and gloves – the Dentdale folk were famed for knitting, but refers to the speed at which their needles moved; that is to say, they knitted terribly quickly. The perspective that needs to be borne in mind is that, for two centuries or more, this dexterity was vital for supplementing a meagre income: speed-knitting was not a party trick, but an indication of dire economic necessity.

We found out more about Dentdale's past through an extremely informative exhibition, 'Discover Dentdale', which is located in a small room that forms part of the tower of Dent's St Andrew's church. Some of the nuggets we picked up from the display include the fact that there was once a mill in Dent which provided marble for the Winter Palace in St Petersburg and that before the First World War Dent boasted nine churches, three banks, two blacksmiths, four butchers, eight boot and shoemakers, two carriers, three coal merchants, two

Valley view of
Dent Head viaduct

fancy goods dealers, three pubs, nine joiners, nine stonemasons, six tailors, eighteen grocers, bakers and confectioners and one hundred and forty-seven farmers. Times have certainly changed – there is now one village store (up for sale), a handful of speciality shops, some inviting-looking cafes and a Post Office which, like so many others in Dales villages, has been earmarked for closure. There is still a blacksmith, though the twenty-first century version is young and female.

Lucy Sandys-Clarke, a blacksmith who works in the forge located close to the village shop, is one of several craftsmen in the dale who are preserving the rural arts while also bringing a modern vision to bear in the application of their skills. An English graduate from Bristol University, thirty-something Lucy has been at the smithy for more than eight years now. Blacksmiths are often associated with shoeing horses: however, Lucy points out that she is not a farrier and would require seven years' specialist training in order to qualify. Nevertheless, her forge is decorated with horseshoes aplenty which dangle from her roof beams, alongside postcards and drawings pegged up on string, which personalise the smithy in an appealing and distinctive manner. '"Blacksmith" is quite a loose term these days,' says Lucy. 'A lot of people work with metal but very few people do traditional blacksmithing which is what I do. I don't use any electricity for welding – it's all done with a coke fire.'

The forge enjoys a history that goes back several centuries – there has been a smithy on the site since about 1640 – and Lucy is happy to be part of that ongoing tradition. She points out one of the anvils which is mounted on an ancient tree stump. 'I often wonder if the forge was built around it,' she says. 'Craft is undervalued today but I think it's really important that we don't lose these traditional skills.'

Inside St Andrew's church you will discover some magnificent stained glass windows and ornate memorials, including one to Adam Sedgwick (1785-1873) which states 'although removed for the greatest part of his life from his beloved birthplace, his love for it was always fresh and he ever revisited it with increasing affection.'

Continuing west beyond Dent on a lane that for much of its length runs parallel with the Dales Way, and is also part of the Yorkshire Cycle Way, you arrive at a junction where by turning left you climb a steep

The River Dee
falls near Cowgill

hill towards the hamlet of Gawthrop along a single-track road. With foxgloves growing alongside the gently winding lane, you begin a journey of rediscovery. This is how life once was, where Man has chosen to live in serene surroundings and well away from the less appealing aspects of urban influences. We looped back towards Dent over a roadbridge near Rash, past the impressive manor house, Gate Manor, continuing back along this wider road and then stopped at what was formerly the Dent Crafts Centre, recently converted into a small exclusive guest house. Originally, the centre served as a combination of gallery, shop, museum and tea rooms. The proprietors, Carrol and Joe Stephenson, had been running the centre for ten years when we met them but, in approaching retirement, have opted to convert the business into a more manageable enterprise. 'We came here from Accrington in Lancashire,' said Carrol. 'We wanted to work and live in this area because it is so beautiful – the landscape is ever-changing. We don't get to walk in it as much as we'd like to, but even when we are working we can see it through the window!' They have so loved their time at the centre and in Dentdale that moving away would have been a wrench. 'We only wished we'd moved here sooner!' says Carrol.

By returning to Dent, you can complete a figure-of-eight journey by heading out of the village towards the south-east and following the lane which leads you back towards Cowgill on the southern side of the Dee. Any perspective on Dentdale is to be prized, especially one that allows you to enjoy what you have already seen from a slightly altered angle. Visiting Dentdale will alter you for the better; and we can guarantee you will want to return there as soon as you can.

Fact File
A Day in a Dale

The Sportsman's Inn
Cowgill, Dent LA10 5RG
☎ 015396 25282
www.thesportsmansinn.com

Dent Station Holiday Cottage
Sleeps six. Contact Robin Hughes
☎ 07824 665266
www.dentstation.co.uk

Dent Village Heritage Centre
Dent, Cumbria LA10 5QJ
☎ 015396 25800
www.dentvillageheritagecentre.com

**High Laning Caravan
and Camping Park**
Dent, nr Sedbergh,
Cumbria LA10 5QJ
☎ 015396 25239
www.highlaning.com

Helmside
Dent, Cumbria LA10 5SY
☎ 015396 25400
*Also Buzzard's Cottage holiday
accommodation is available nearby*

Yewgales camping and caravan site
☎ 015396 25440

Meadowside cafe bar
The Laning, Dent,
Cumbria LA10 5QJ
☎ 015396 25329
www.dentdale.com/meadowside
*Also available is the Old Sunday School
two person studio accommodation*

Blacksmith
Lucy Sandys-Clarke
www.lucysandysclarke.com

The late afternoon
sunshine escapes
Snaizeholme

THE RED SQUIRREL DALE
Widdale (August)

Each of our days spent exploring a dale inevitably has involved a car journey getting us there and back within daylight hours. The further we roam as this series has continued, the more obvious it is that a day is never quite enough, and that the car is only a means to a limited end – travelling on foot would be infinitely preferable, with overnight accommodation a subsequent necessity. If you happen to find yourself near Hawes with some hours to spare, by all means use your car to explore Widdale and neighbouring dales as already described, but seriously contemplate abandoning your vehicle on a regular basis to enjoy these dales' delights on foot.

We made for Appersett, near Hawes, on the A684 route to Sedburgh. This small hamlet (whose name, derived from the original Norse, means either the farm or the pasture next to the apple tree – those Vikings were truly poetic as well as keen-eyed in ascribing place names) has only twenty three dwellings, though there is a haulage depot on the outskirts, and an art gallery. The Artbar Gallery exhibits the work of Moira Metcalfe, an artist who is also a farmer's wife. Though she works using different media – oils, watercolour on silk, watercolours and pastels – it is her colourful depictions of the local landscape using oils which really catch the eye.

A Day In A Dale

'I am very influenced by my surroundings,' says Moira. 'I couldn't imagine living anywhere else. I love it here. The landscape is endlessly inspirational and the light you get around here is fantastic.' Moira also offers courses in painting, including for beginners, through her association with the nearby Stone House Hotel on the other side of the River Ure. What characterises Moira's oil paintings is her sense of seemingly abstract shape inspired by the contours of the landscape and local features – dry-stone walls and field-barns – often represented in non-naturalistic or exaggerated blends of colour.

The village green at Appersett is small and practical, with several washing lines on display, though the washing had been taken in on the (mainly dry) day of our visit. Nearby is the stone-built road bridge over the Widdale Beck, no great distance from the confluence with the River Ure. Appersett is an excellent starting point for walks to the village of Hardraw, with its famous falls, the largest single drop waterfall in England, and into tucked-away Cotter Dale, with the opportunity to climb high up onto Great Shunner Fell from where the views in all directions are magnificent.

We left Appersett on the easily missable Lanacer Lane, just to the east of the bridge. (We were part way to Sedburgh before we realised we'd missed it). Without any doubt, this is the most visually appealing stretch of Widdale, the name meaning 'the wooded valley' in Old Norse. The beck tumbles down a steep wooded ravine, bisected quite beautifully by the Appersett Viaduct, part of the now defunct branch line between Hawes and Garsdale which once linked with the Settle-Carlisle railway. Half a mile further on look out for Thorney Mire Barn, its name being the least attractive aspect of a very appealing luxury bed and breakfast establishment – with not a thorn or mire in sight. Owned since 2004 by Simon and Jane Hudson, it has built up a considerable reputation amongst those for whom a single day in this area is simply not long enough.

When the lane runs out, it joins the relatively busy B6255, one of the trunk roads that joins Hawes and Settle. Forestry plantations here might seem a temporary blot on the landscape with industrial-scale felling currently taking place. However, the remaining conifers are also now a reserve for the protection of red squirrels, the five separate mini-forests together forming one of only two reserves in Yorkshire dedicated to this purpose (the other being located at nearby Garsdale and Mallerstang). Reserves elsewhere in Northern England are located in substantial, continuous forests unlike the patchwork nature of the Widdale plantations. Nevertheless they were chosen because it does offer an important opportunity to encourage the geographical range of reds remaining on the mainland in England. It is probably true to say that only very recently have people, even locally, become aware that red squirrels are present in significant numbers in this area of Yorkshire.

In October 2008, the Red Squirrel Trail was launched – a ten-mile walking route from the Dales Countryside Museum in Hawes up to woodland near Snaizeholme – which allows walkers to catch a glimpse of these shy, winsome creatures. The trail was set up, in partnership with the Yorkshire Dales National Park and the Save Our Squirrels project in Cumbria, by local forester Hugh Kemp, a former Christmas tree grower, who owns an eighteenth century farmhouse in the vicinity. The areas of woodland he has planted over the past forty years now form part of the Widdale Red Squirrel Reserve. The trail goes through specially planted woodland that is attractive to red squirrels and where increasing numbers are now frequently observed. There is also the possibility of spotting other forms of wildlife: roe deer, for example, are regular visitors round these parts as well as pine martens.

Grey squirrels outnumber the native British red by a ratio of sixty six to one but, through careful woodland management, this could change – as Hugh has demonstrated. Greys are attracted to sycamores and oaks, so Hugh undertook a programme of sycamore and oak removal, replacing them with willows, which attract reds, and larch. Larch cones are, according to Hugh, a particular favourite with reds. He has also put up feeding boxes containing peanuts, sunflower seeds and pine kernels. Specially commissioned squirrel dormitories provide a safe haven for reds to spend the night, especially since the aperture is specifically designed to be too small for greys to enter. Over twelve hundred native trees and shrubs have been planted, including a natural willow hedge in front of the squirrel viewing area on the footpath which helps to 'hide' people from the shy creatures. There are signs and explanatory leaflets all along the way.

Anyone who is interested in doing the walk should visit The

Over the wall
in Widdale

Yorkshire Dales National Park authority office in Hawes where the helpful staff will provide further information, leaflets and maps. There is no charge to go on the walk, but if a group would like a guided tour through the woodland, Hugh is always very happy to do that, by appointment, for which there is a small charge.

Continuing south, allow your eye to drift westwards towards Widdale Fell, the summit of which is the appealingly-named Great Knoutberry Hill, on the sides of which coal was mined in past centuries. The dale widens out (perhaps Widdale should mean 'the wide dale') over this stretch the further you rise and the vista suddenly surprises you with a distant view of the distinctive shape of Ingleborough.

In our original article for the *Yorkshire Post* we included Upper Dentdale as part of our day out and the two dales combine superbly especially if railway viaducts hold particular appeal to you. On this particular day we visited Widdale from north to south, when most tourists would almost certainly approach from the direction of the Ribblehead Viaduct (providing the opportunity to see four magnificent

Bridge over
Widdale Beck

viaducts in a matter of just a few miles, three of them viewable from the roadside). Either way, the dale is a good example of how all too easy it is for car drivers to use a route as a means of getting from A to B and fail to discover the delights that lie just off the main road for those who choose to explore a little further and a little more deeply.

Fact File

A Day in a Dale

Moira Metcalfe, Artbar Gallery
Nether Bar East, Appersett, Hawes,
North Yorkshire DL8 3LN
☎ 01969 667782
www.artbargallery.co.uk

Stone House Hotel
Sedbusk, near Hawes,
North Yorkshire DL8 3PT
☎ 01969 667571
www.stonehousehotel.co.uk

Thorney Mire Barn
Appersett, Hawes,
North Yorkshire DL8 3LU
☎ 01969 666122
www.thorneymirebarn.co.uk

Save our Squirrels Project
c/o Cumbria Wildlife Trust
Alaska Building, Penrith CA11 7EH
☎ 01768 212521
www.saveoursquirrels.org.uk

The unmistakeable
landscape of
Ingleborough

THE 'AWAY FROM IT ALL' DALE
Chapel le Dale (March)

In days gone by the road through Chapel le Dale would have been a significant thoroughfare linking Ingleton, already on a major road, with Yorkshire settlements to the north and east, particularly Hawes and Richmond, both towns which feature on the regular milestones in the dale. In such mountainous terrain, level and fairly straight routes through the wilds must have been a blessing, so it's small wonder to find a bridge over the Chapel Beck known as God's Bridge. The Romans discovered this passageway for themselves, though the old Roman road runs on the other side of the River Doe and Chapel Beck from the modern B road.

Visitors to Chapel le Dale – and there are thousands of them, mainly because of the popularity of White Scar Cave, though there are plenty of other reasons for coming here – benefit from returning on more than one occasion. The weather is, of course, variable and it would be quite possible to journey the length of the dale in cloud or mist and not appreciate that the valley is flanked by two of Yorkshire's three great peaks, Whernside and Ingleborough. Return on a clear day, however, and the views are joyous, views that will demand you put on your hiking boots and stride out.

White Scar Cave is the longest show cave tour in the UK, covering over a mile (half a mile there and half a mile back) underground. With around seventy thousand visitors a year, it's one of Yorkshire's major tourist attractions and rewards stopping off to take the eighty minute guided tour – a perfect activity if the weather is dull or cold. The cave is open year round, only shutting if there is flooding inside the cave. Our friendly and informative guide Chris Hudson told us that even the heavy snowfall that winter hadn't prevented them from opening. 'We got to work and thought we might have a day off as the entrance was almost covered by thick snow,' he says, laughing, 'but then we got the shovels out and it was business as usual.'

The cave was discovered in 1923 by Cambridge undergraduate and amateur geologist Christopher Long. 'He was on holiday with a friend in the area and the whole purpose of their stay was to find new cave systems,' explains our guide Chris. 'For light all he had was a bowler hat with three candles strapped to it.' In 1924, the cave was opened to the public, although not via the tiny entrance that Long had crawled through. Blasting and tunnelling was carried out by unemployed miners from Ingleton to create a tunnel high enough for a six foot person to walk along comfortably. Since then concrete pathways and bridges have been added as the system has been opened further for the public. Hard hats are provided and although most of the tour can be done walking comfortably upright, there are sections where bending almost double is required. The Gorilla Walk is so-named because, though well-protected by the hard hats, the best way to avoid striking one's head on the tunnel's rocky roof is to adopt the posture of an inelegant ape for seventy or so yards.

One of the most impressive features on the tour is an underground waterfall which can be heard thundering and echoing long before it comes into view. It is hard to imagine attempting to climb up such a flow of water that gushes down into a deep pool from quite a height and with a great deal of force, but that is precisely what Christopher Long did in 1923 in order to exit the cave. It was at this point on the tour that another member of our party asked whether the cave ever flooded and Chris replied with a wry smile, 'Well... I normally leave the flood talk until we are on the way out.' He left it at that and we continued (somewhat nervously) on our way.

Our next stop was at The Sword of Damocles, a twenty-thousand year-old stalactite which does indeed look like a huge broadsword. Chris told us that 'some bright spark', as he politely put it, had tried to steal the sword some years ago. They had managed to break it away from the ceiling of the cave but had then abandoned it in a stream on their way out. Luckily it had been found and was wired back in to place. Eventually the process of flowstone and stalactite formation will cover up the repair job but it will take time. 'If you come back in four or five hundred years' time, it should look good as new,' quipped Chris.

The tour ends at the awe-inspiring Battlefield Cavern – so-called because the rubble of rocks in one corner suggests the aftermath of explosive warfare. This magnificent cave – nine metres long and thirty metres tall at its highest point – was discovered by nineteen-year-old Hilda Guthrie in 1971. 'Hilda was part of a caving group called The Happy Wanderers,' says Chris indicating a mannequin dressed in waterproof gear standing next to a small pothole. 'That's where she came through – she was the only woman in the group and the men, being gentlemen, sent her ahead first.' Serene silence prevails – elsewhere in the cave system there is the constant sound of running water from the subterranean streams and waterfalls but here it is perfectly, eerily, quiet. As we head back, Chris tells us that Hilda came on a tour some years ago, unannounced, and only revealed who she was when the tour leader referred to the mannequin – at which point she laughed and said: 'That's me!'

On leaving the cave, we headed up the valley to the charming little hamlet of Chapel le Dale to visit St Leonard's church, a tiny chapel, located in a woodland dell, which dates back to the seventeenth century and is only forty-eight feet long and twenty-two feet wide. As you leave the main road and park up in the church car park, it will feel as if a green filter has been put over your eyes – moss clings to every available rocky surface or tree. If ever you were to hope to find elves or fairies, this green grotto would be the place to start looking.

Delightful as the setting is, the church of St Leonard's, celebrated by artists such as Turner who knew Chapel le Dale as Ingleton Fells, has a more sonorous history as the graveyard of many of those who died during the construction of the nearby Ribblehead Viaduct during the 1870s. Sadly, those who fell victim to the hardships of the navvying

A Day In A Dale

The solitary
splendour of
Whernside

work were not only the labourers but also their wives and children, around two hundred in all, who succumbed to diseases while living in harsh and unforgiving conditions. The original plaque inside the church makes no reference to the women and their offspring, an omission now acknowledged by a more recent commemoration in the graveyard, close to the burial place of these unfortunate guests of the dale, now permanent residents.

Chapel le Dale is fine hiking country and the church is a good place to start a walk. Our advice would be to tackle Ingleborough, if you only have time for one climb, which will provide a true appreciation of the delights of the dale. As you cross through pasture land strewn with limestone boulders, gradually ascending towards a peak of seven hundred and twenty-three metres atop Ingleborough's characteristic slanting plateau, the views along the dale become breathtaking. The hamlet of Chapel le Dale shyly hides amongst its surrounding trees; the Ribblehead Viaduct, at the head of the dale, paces across the landscape, pointing your gaze towards the whaleback of Whernside; to the south and west, there are gentler terrains in view towards the Lune Valley and beyond. If the skies are clear enough, you will see as far as to Morecambe Bay in the west as well as enjoying uninterrupted views towards the smallest, but perhaps most dramatic, of the Three Peaks, Pen-y-ghent, due east.

Along the walk, you will encounter an astonishing mix of landscapes: tree-lined fields where sheep graze, limestone pavements, pot-holes and gullies (including the crater-like and curiously-named Braithwaite Wife Hole); you will cross marshy terrain on boardwalks and mount a seemingly endless staircase of rock before the hugely rewarding final stretches of the ascent. And while we would often advise a circular route on any walk, returning to Chapel le Dale by retracing one's steps will provide you with the constant pleasure of views northwards that you will only have appreciated occasionally while catching your breath on the outward leg.

Once back down to Chapel le Dale, if you head onto the main road in the direction of the Ribblehead Viaduct you will soon come to The Old Hill Inn, a charming, ancient hostelry dating back to 1615. Although we visited on a Monday, the one day of the week the inn is closed, we were nevertheless offered a very warm welcome by Colin and Sabeena Martin who have been running the establishment for ten years or so. They have built up a fine gastronomic reputation in that time – not surprising since the Martins are a family of accomplished chefs. Sabeena, Colin and two of their three children are all experts in the culinary arts and glowing reviews on the wall attest to their skills. 'We get mostly walkers during the day,' says Sabeena. 'Then in the evenings we have people coming from quite a distance: Bradford, Leeds, Skipton, Dent, Sedbergh, Lancaster. There's even a man who comes over from Manchester just for the puds!'

Making a mental note to pop back for a meal sometime, we crossed the road to the Old School Bunkhouse where we met the friendly owner, Clare Fox. Clare and her husband Peter, who live in Settle, have owned the bunkhouse which sleeps up to thirty people, for more than three years now. 'We love the countryside here; you really do feel as though you are "away from it all",' says Clare. 'My husband and I used to come up here on trips when we were at Foxwood School in Leeds in the seventies – and when the chance to buy the bunkhouse came up, we went for it. It's something we've always wanted to do.'

Chapel le Dale gained its name from its chapel of ease. There's no doubt that today's visitors to the dale will find themselves at ease, renewed and re-energised by its peace, beauty and tranquillity.

Fact File

A Day in a Dale

White Scar Cave
Ingleton, North Yorkshire LA6 3AW
☎ 015242 41244
Open daily February to October and weekends November to January (weather permitting)
🖰 www.whitescarcave.co.uk

The Old Hill Inn
Chapel-le-Dale,
North Yorkshire LA6 3AR
☎ 015242 41256
🖰 www.oldhillinn.co.uk

The Old School Bunkhouse
Chapel le Dale, Ingleton,
North Yorkshire LA6 3AR
☎ 01729 823835 ☏ 07801 979945
🖰 www.oldschoolbunkhouse.co.uk

Croft Gate Bed and Breakfast
Chapel le Dale, Ingleton,
North Yorkshire LA6 3JG
☎ 01524 242664
🖰 www.croft-gate.co.uk

A chimney stands
proud in Settle

THE DRAMATIC DALE
Ribblesdale (July)

There are many approaches to Settle to begin a day in one of
Yorkshire's most dramatic dales. The route we chose was from Airton
along Scotsthrop Lane, a single track with passing places. It's not long,
if you travel this way, before you feel as if you've left civilisation
behind, with not a dwelling, other than the odd field barn, in sight for
miles around.

We did, however, encounter a Postbus – a delivery van doubling as
public transport – a sensible, environmentally friendly idea; we also
saw a cheery, lone cyclist smiling brightly as he rounded a bend,
despite the unseasonably cool and damp weather.

Sheep frequently share the unfenced moorland with cattle. One
small herd of Highland cows seemed quite comfortable on the lane
itself. Peering at us through their long ginger fringes, one shaggy
creature, its mane and flanks the colour of Irn Bru, was friendly (or
inquisitive) enough to poke his head in at the passenger window and
to have a lick of the wing mirror.

One of the reasons for approaching Ribblesdale by this route is to
enjoy the roadside waterfall of Scaleber Force. A few steps after
crossing the stile towards a small copse, you find yourself gazing down
upon an impressive torrent, powerful yet elegant, curving in its

cascades. The summer's wet weather meant that the water was certainly falling with some force, best appreciated by following the steep path down into the glade of trees that surround the falls. So steep are the slopes that it seems miraculous that the mixture of deciduous and pine trees are able to cling to the sides without toppling into the gully beneath. Some have given up the struggle to hang on and there were many fallen trees, whose roots reached skywards like crazy branches of Medusa's hair. In damp conditions, the steps down can be treacherous, so please take care.

The steep descent into Settle feels reminiscent of an episode of *Last of the Summer Wine*, though Holmfirth is many miles to the south near the border with Derbyshire. You enter the older part of the town by means of an attractive narrow lane – part of which is still cobbled – that transports you into former times, a sensation that continues as you encounter The Folly. This remarkable seventeenth century manor house, now a museum and five star holiday accommodation, stands on what was, in days gone by, the main road into the town and attracts plenty of tourists, as does the market square. Every view is presided over by Low High Hill, Middle High Hill and High Hill, ever-present limestone-outcrop reminders that this is a dales town.

We came in search of the River Ribble and its dale: Settle, however, gives the impression of having turned its back on the river which serves as a boundary between itself and its western neighbour, Giggleswick. It's almost as if the townsfolk feel slightly embarrassed that their waterway is the only major Yorkshire river which ultimately flows west into Lancashire rather than following the more usual course south and eastwards towards the Humber.

From Settle we headed north, albeit with a brief stop to photograph the weir, where the natural colouring of the iron-rich and peaty waters make the Ribble look like beer on tap. We didn't get much further before stopping at the Watershed Mill, its tall and impressive chimney a remnant of its 1820s origins. It was once a cotton mill ('a long time since' according to one of the ladies behind the till), but is now a retail outlet and coffee shop which also sells bottled Yorkshire ales (assuming it's not just bottled Ribble water).

Heading north towards Stainforth and beyond, what distinguishes Ribblesdale from all of the other dales we have visited is the constant

A train makes its way over Ribblesdale's famous viaduct

awareness of the three r's – the river, the road and the railway. The B6479 is a relatively major highway for a Yorkshire dale; the railway follows one of the most famous rail routes in the country; and the river is an ever-variable, gradually dwindling watercourse as one traces it (as far as is possible) to its source.

Just to the west of the charming little village of Stainforth, and just east of the even littler Little Stainforth, are the only significant falls of this section of the river. Don't attempt to park close to Stainforth Force – the road here is about as narrow as a road can be while still allowing a single vehicle to squeeze over the packbridge, and double yellow lines, somewhat incongruously in this rural setting, forbid any opportunity to save the legs of the lazy or the weary. Best to park in one of the nearby villages and savour a riverside walk you are unlikely to forget.

A little to the north, you come to a divergence in the road at Helwith Bridge, the route west taking you towards Austwick, the road north towards the unmissable Horton-in-Ribblesdale. Apart from the pub at Helwith (appropriately named the Helwith Bridge Inn), it's the bridge you want to pay attention to; it's unusual in that it crosses both the river and the railway in its span.

Horton-in-Ribbledale is deservedly famous as the centre of the Three Peaks Challenge, the renowned Pen-y-ghent Café being the start and finish point, with its clocking-in ticket punch machine allowing you twelve hours to complete the trek up Pen-y-ghent itself, and Ingleborough and Whernside in whichever order you choose. Starting or finishing, it's a good location, serving promptly-delivered hot meals and tea in pint mugs. Walkers will find every book and map imaginable to aid them here, or merino wool socks at bargain prices. Quirky and amusing signs adorn the walls, including one which proclaims this to be 'a mobile free zone' adding 'If your phone rings, proceed quickly to the outside porch.'

Friendly proprietor Melanie Bayes explained that her family have run the café since 1965 and that she has been serving behind the counter on and off since she was a little girl. 'When my parents retired recently, I came back to help in the running of the place for a while,' she said. Melanie has lived 'all over the place – Gloucestershire, Scotland, India.' What was it like for her to return? 'Well, I suppose you see things in a different way when you come back,'

A tunnel sits snugly beneath the railway and Pen-y-ghent

Ribblesdale

she mused. 'There are lots of things I value about Yorkshire that I perhaps didn't when I was younger.'

Horton is a deceptive village. When you enter it from the south, you might be tempted to think it's a tiny place as you encounter St Oswald's Church (with its fourteenth century tower and Norman nave) and the Golden Lion hotel and pub before running out of dwellings. But then there's a bit more to the north, particularly the Crown Inn by the bridge and the bend, where a tributary converges with the Ribble. From here there are lovely views of Pen-y-ghent. Then, there's more again at the next bend, including the railway station which deposits so many of the shorts-and-boots-clad walkers ready to make their taxing triple ascents.

Further to the north is the tiny hamlet of Selside, one of the few houses there boldly proclaiming the name from whichever direction you approach. If you are driving, as we were, it's all too easy to pass through a place like Selside without noticing quite how enchanting the houses are – hidden away architectural treasures whose owners share in a portion of paradise. Not far from here, where Gayle Beck and Cam Beck converge, is often taken to be the source of the Ribble, though accounts vary. Close to Selside the landscape is made up of low rolling hillocks on either side of the road; as we drove we also noticed what becomes a regular feature, little tunnels under the railway track permitting access to the fields beyond for farmer and stock alike.

Looking to the left, the distinctive peak of Ingleborough is now a prominent shape upon the near horizon. In time you reach a T junction. Turning right, you head north-east towards Hawes on the Blea Moor Road. Turning left, you follow the Low Sleights Road a tiny distance to the Station Inn where the weary traveller can find good beer, accommodation and home cooked food. Hanging from a chain on the outside wall is the entertaining Weather Forecasting Stone which offers up such words of meteorological wisdom as 'stone is wet: it's raining', 'stone is dry: it's not raining', 'stone is white: it's snowing', 'can't see stone: it's foggy'.

Whatever the weather, however, even if long-distance views are not on the agenda, you can't miss the gigantic, imposing structure of the Ribblehead Viaduct with its twenty-four arches. This hugely impressive man-made feature, perhaps the most photographed stretch of railway-line anywhere in the world and on the most dramatic section of the Settle-Carlisle railway, is now open again after recent repair work.

The station houses an informative museum about the viaduct and its construction. The Settle-Carlisle railway itself was the last manually-built railway and, at the height of the building work, seven thousand men were employed, with two thousand on the viaduct alone. A photograph taken at the time of the building of the viaduct shows the shanty towns built for the workers in the background. One area was known as Belgravia – where the management lived – and another was known as San Sebastopol.

During July and August on Sundays and Wednesdays during the time of the repair work guided walks took place on the viaduct. Paul Kampen, one of the guides, said that the walks had proved to be very popular but have now had to be halted because the trains are running again. As we looked out at the grim, wet weather of a damp July, Paul commented wryly: 'It's like that old Yorkshire saying: if you can see the hills it's going to rain, if you can't, it's raining.'

The weir in full flow at Settle

The curve of the Ribblehead Viaduct

A quick glance at the visitors' book during our visit revealed that recent visitors to the station had come from Norway, Tasmania, Australia, Scotland, Norfolk, Wiltshire, Canada, South Africa and Taiwan. There seemed to be a lot of visitors from Norfolk and it soon became apparent to us why after talking to station warden Mike Neal. He and his wife Rosey had moved up from Norfolk. 'We used to come up here a lot on holiday,' he explained, 'and we got to know the people who were wardens here. They retired, we applied for the job and we got it.' Their move up north wasn't without problems though, since a month after their arrival Mike had a massive heart attack. 'It's lovely here and the people are wonderful. While I was recovering everyone was really helpful, coming round to see if we needed anything.'

A fan of railways, Mike first visited the viaduct more than thirty-five years ago. 'If you'd have told me then that one day I'd be living in the station as a warden, I wouldn't have believed you, but you never know what life's going to throw at you.' In fact, partly because of health issues, Mike and Rosey returned to Norfolk a few months later, their place being taken by Tony and Pat Beckwith for the subsequent two years. Keen supporters of the Settle-Carlisle trust, the Beckwiths will be continuing to volunteer their assistance even after retiring, whilst, at the time of writing, the future of the Visitors Centre will be decided by the trust.

Looking at displays on the walls, there was a surprising photograph of the viaduct which clearly showed its curvature, not at all apparent when you look at it face on. Also, the southern end is lower than the northern end by at least twelve feet. We recommend walking along the bridleway to the foot of the viaduct itself to appreciate the scale of this towering brickwork, completed by 1875 though at the cost of many lives.

At any time of year, there'll be a tea bar at the T junction – with cars parked on the verges to appreciate the view in all directions. And what a view! From here you can (even on a cloudy day) see all three of the famous peaks within one sweeping glance in one of the most impressive viewing points in the whole of Yorkshire.

Fact File

**The Watershed Mill
and Visitor Centre**
Langcliffe Road, Settle,
North Yorkshire
☎ 01729 825539
www.watershedmill.co.uk

Pen-y-ghent Café
Horton-in-Ribblesdale,
North Yorkshire BD24 OHE
☎ 01729 860333
www.pen-y-ghentcafe.co.uk

The Golden Lion Hotel
Horton-in-Ribblesdale,
North Yorkshire BD24 0HB
☎ 01729 860206
www.goldenlionhotel.co.uk

The Station Inn
Ribblehead,
North Yorkshire LA6 3AS
☎ 01524 241274
www.thestationinn.net

**Ribblehead Viaduct
and station visitors' centre**
☎ 01524 242584
www.settle-carlisle.com

The Helwith Bridge Inn
www.helwithbridge.com

The Folly at Settle
Settle, North Yorkshire BD24 9EY
☎ 01729 822930
www.follysettle.co.uk

Malham attracts
visitors galore -
and livestock!

THE FRIENDLY - AND AWE-INSPIRING - DALE
Malhamdale (June)

All roads lead to Rome, they say. That's as maybe, but two or three of them pass through Malham en route, and they are some of the loveliest roads you will find west of the Seven Hills.

Our favourite approach is from the north, simply because it provides another excuse to see Littondale. You fork off at Arncliffe on the road that runs alongside Cowside Beck, one of the most beautiful and dramatic lanes to be found anywhere in the Dales. Look out for the dry stone walls that run precipitously – and somewhat perplexingly – up the severe slope towards Yew Cogar Scar.

Beyond Darnbrook House (approached by the hairiest of hairpin bends) you come to Thoragill Beck where it is worth taking some time to acquaint yourself with the ancient stone bridge (intrepid young explorers can pass beneath it without necessarily stepping into the water) and to listen to the lulling burble of the beck.

Near Home Farm, as Malham Tarn hoves into view, there is a sizeable lay-by where those who want to take advantage of recently-established walks can park. The Yorkshire Dales National Park, along with English Nature, English Heritage and the Countryside Commission, has teamed up with local landowners to give access to a wider range of Malham Moor than was previously available to walkers. Leaflets giving further details can be obtained from the National Park Centre on the southern outskirts of Malham.

East of the Tarn, the road is joined by the Henside Road from Ribblesdale, a route enjoyed by the more enterprising motorist. The likelier approach is from the A65, to the south of Malham, turning off at Gargrave. You pass the elegant Eshton Hall (now converted into luxury apartments and cottages) set in a verdant parkland landscape reminiscent of the approach to Bolton Abbey from Addingham. Look out also for Newfield Hall, just before the picturesque village of Airton, where stylish country accommodation provided by HF Holidays is offered. Heading north, you enter (and will scarcely want to leave) the

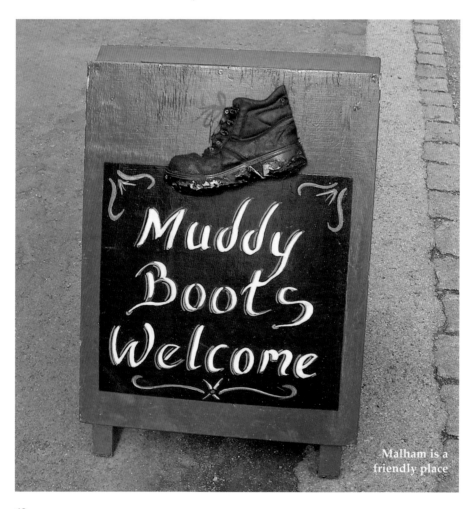

Malham is a friendly place

beautiful village of Kirkby Malham, with its medieval church, charming stone cottages and its inviting pub, the Victoria Inn.

Heading further north, the impression created is of entering a circle of hills (not seven, as in Rome, but commanding nonetheless, and Kirkby Fell the most dominant at nearly two thousand feet), with side valleys leading off in various directions. However, even before the collection of farms and dwellings that make up Malham itself can clearly be seen, the great geological amphitheatre of the cove dramatically announces its presence.

On arrival in the village, there are options for parking (on the roadside, or in a local farmer's field opened up on busy days, for example) but the most sensible place is at the National Park visitors centre pay and display car park. It is also advisable to go into the centre and pick up a few of the informative leaflets about walks, cycle rides and drives in the area. Most of them are available either free or for a small fee.

The centre also offers some insight into the response of artists and writers over the years to Malham and its surrounding landscape. These include Turner, Wordsworth, WH Auden and, more recently, Bill Bryson, who lived and worked in Kirkby Malham for several years. He is quoted as saying that Malhamdale is 'the finest place there is' although he reserved judgement, not having yet seen heaven.

The overall impression that the exhibition conveys is that the early visitors to the area were awe-inspired – in the sense of being filled with dread – by the overpowering quality of the landscape. Accessibility in the modern age has perhaps conspired to reduce the impact on today's visitors. The contrast is all too apparent in the nonetheless admirable policy of Malhamdale's marketers to promote the area as 'the Friendly Dale'.

It's a good idea to abandon your car in Malham as there are so many walks to enjoy which start from the village. The Malhamdale Initiative, who have their own website, have published a free leaflet detailing five splendid walks in and around Malham, incorporating the Tarn, the Cove, Gordale Scar, Janet's Foss and local villages. All five walks, varying in length from three and a half to eight miles, make partial use of the Pennine Way which passes from south to north, directly past the Cove, and then strikes east from Malham Tarn.

A Day In A Dale

The dramatic
sight of
Malham Cove

A Day In A Dale

The enchanted - and enchanting - waterfall of Janet's Foss

Walkers who enjoy more of a challenge might consider trying the somewhat inappropriately titled Malham Meander – a twenty three mile circular route from Kirby Malham with badges and certificates awarded to those who complete the course within ten hours. This is an annual event which takes place in May and there is a small registration fee. For those who would prefer a shorter walk, there is the Mini Meander which is nine and a half miles. There is information about both walks on the Malhamdale website.

One of the walks from Malham takes you up to Gordale Scar, following the beck through woodland. As the trail is about to join up with the road again and the woodland section of the walk comes to an end, you encounter the enchanting (if not enchanted) waterfall of Janet's Foss, with its pool, cave and mystical associations. Janet (or Jennet) was, according to legend, the Queen of the Fairies and said to live in the small cave behind the falls. Be careful of your step here for fear the falls will come to be named after you.

Gordale Scar was once an enormous cavern which collapsed to create the present-day gorge. In contrast to Malham Cove, which with its cathedral-like stature almost brashly demands your attention, Gordale Scar, though equally massive, is more subtly seductive, gradually drawing you into its narrowing cliff-wall secrets. Not surprisingly, few can resist the urge to clamber up beyond its waterfall to the path leading north and westwards to Malham Tarn.

The Tarn is the largest natural lake in Yorkshire, though part of its size is due to damming which took place in the late eighteenth century. It's approximately half a mile in diameter, with a surface area of one hundred and fifty acres. On its northern shore your eye will be drawn to Tarn House (which is now a National Trust visitors and field study centre) and the nearby folly. There are many who believe that the weir that feeds the stream on the southern shoreline is the source of the River Aire. However, this beck disappears through sink holes after a short distance and the true source of Leeds' famous watercourse (at least in terms of surface water) is to be found at Aire Head, a little to the south of the village of Malham. Controversy still surrounds the precise underground source.

The pubs and cafes of Malham are ideal either for those seeking rest and refreshment after a day of rambling, as well as for those who feel no need of a ten-mile hike to work up a healthy thirst and appetite. The pub you're most likely to spot first is the Buck Inn, but don't neglect the Lister Arms, a seventeenth century inn (listed in *The Good Beer Guide*) which is located off the green on the lane to Gordale Scar.

Muddy boots are welcomed at The Old Barn Café; there was a coffee shop at the Cove Centre which also sold country clothing and accessories (but which appeared to have closed down on our last visit); our favourite spot for a bite and a cuppa, however, is Beck Hall where you can feed your crusts to the ducks who visit you at your table when they are not paddling in the adjacent beck. For other friendly creatures, both feathered and furry, you could treat the children or yourselves to a trip to the Malham Visitor Farm on the southern edge of the village.

The day out needn't be over yet. If you wanted to vary your route home, you might consider driving through Calton, looking out for Calton Hall where John Lambert, a prominent architect of the Cromwellian Protectorate and, according to the plaque, 'a man of extraordinary parts', was born in 1619.

Make Hetton your target and you will pass through the delightful hamlet of Winterburn en route and find yourself in what feels like Tolkien country, with the distinctive and unusual peaks of Cracoe Fell and Hall Fell as your eastern backdrop. On the day of our visit, we were more than minorly entertained to witness a Morris Minor convention taking part in a rally between Scarborough and Morecambe. None of the drivers, as far as we could see, were hobbits.

The main reason for heading for Hetton is to stop at the Angel Inn, an award-winning pub and restaurant with one of the finest reputations for good food in the North of England – if not the entire country. If you're with a good friend, where better to spend an evening after a day in 'The Friendly Dale'?

Fact File

A Day in a Dale

Gordale Scar campsite
Malham, Skipton
North Yorkshire BD23 4DL
☎ 01729 830333
www.malhamdale.com/camping

The Buck Inn
Malham, Nr Skipton,
North Yorkshire BD23 4DA
☎ 01729 830317
www.buckinnmalham.co.uk

The Lister Arms Hotel
Malham, Nr Skipton,
North Yorkshire BD23 4DB
☎ 01729 830330
www.lister-arms.co.uk

Malham Meander
for further details visit
www.malhamdale.com

Beck Hall
Malham, Nr Skipton,
North Yorkshire BD23 4DJ
☎ 01729 830332
www.beckhallmalham.com

The Angel at Hetton
Hetton, nr Skipton,
North Yorkshire BD23 6LT
☎ 01756 730263
www.angelhetton.co.uk

Malham Youth Hostel
☎ 01729 830321
www.yha.co.uk

Newfield Hall
Airton, Malhamdale,
North Yorkshire BD23 4AA
☎ 01729 830235
www.hfholidays.co.uk

WENSLEYDALE AND NEIGHBOURS

Garsdale, Grisedale, Cotter Dale,
Wensleydale, Raydale, Apedale

The view from
Garsdale station

THE DALE OF THE CLOUGH
Garsdale (April)

On a day of dramatically changeable weather – there was hail, rain, sunshine and spectacular rainbows – we headed out to explore Garsdale, a valley through which the A684 road runs from Sedbergh to Hawes. There can be few main roads in the country quite as quiet as the A684, and driving along it allows the opportunity to enjoy magnificent scenery at the same time as delving back into a fascinating, if at times tragic, history.

An oddity of the journey is that between the two towns you will find only one watering-hole – there's no café, pub, shop or restaurant for most of the sixteen mile stretch other than the Moorcock Inn, which is at the junction of Garsdale Head and Mallerstang, the valley that leads you north to Kirkby Stephen. You'd be well advised to call in here anyway, even if it wasn't the only pub in Garsdale, for the warmth of the welcome offered by its publicans, Simon Tijou and Caz Field.

Simon's unusual French surname can be traced back to a Jean Tijou who came over from France in the seventeenth century. 'He did all the wrought iron work at St Paul's Cathedral,' says Simon. Caz's family are Yorkshire folk and the couple originally moved up from the south to be nearer Caz's parents who are based in Carperby. Having decided they would like to run a pub together, Simon and Caz started looking in the area and the Moorcock Inn came up as a freehold property. 'As soon as we walked in, we knew we wanted to run this place,' says Simon.

Their customers are made up of walkers, holidaymakers and locals. 'It's surprising the number of people who live within two or three miles of here,' says Simon. 'There isn't a definite centre to Garsdale – it is quite spread out, but there is still a community feeling about it.' And the pub itself is an important part of that sense of community. According to Simon there has been some sort of inn on the site for centuries, but the present building dates back to the 1740s, although one section has been replaced after a fire in 1975 in which the then owners died. A framed newspaper article on the wall relates the story and, although it has never been ascertained what actually happened, the locals have their own theories. 'A lot of people round here think that the couple did it on purpose,' says Simon. 'They were elderly, in their seventies, and they had just been refused a licence. Apparently they had told someone that the only way they would be leaving the pub was 'in a box''. So it appears that it may have been a suicide pact.

Garsdale Hall

Given this grisly history, had Simon seen any ghosts in the pub? He is hesitant in his reply ('I don't really believe in that kind of thing, but…') and then relates a couple of 'weird things that have happened.' Getting up after their first night at the pub, Simon and Caz noticed that furniture had been moved around in the bar. On another occasion not long after they moved in, Simon decided to get all the fire extinguishers replaced. 'When the guy arrived and announced who he was and where he was from, the framed newspaper article fell off the wall and the glass smashed. I don't know if it was just a coincidence, but it really freaked me out for a couple of days.'

Another potentially spooky fact about the pub is that when the St Pancras to Glasgow express collided with a pair of light engines on Christmas Eve 1910 near the Dandry Mire viaduct (just behind the inn) the bodies of the twelve victims were stored in the pub's cellar. The dead were later buried in the small churchyard at Hawes. Doesn't Simon ever feel nervous about going down into the cellar? 'No, never. It always feels really warm and friendly here. If there are any ghosts around, they are nice ones.'

Much of the history of this part of the Dales is inextricably linked with the railways. At one time Garsdale Head was known as Hawes Junction because of the branch line from the Settle-Carlisle line which extended all the way along Wensleydale. There's regular rail traffic passing through Garsdale on England's most scenic stretch of track, punctuated by viaducts, bridges and tunnels – so it's small wonder that the Rev W Awdry was so inspired by the area. His son is a patron of the Wensleydale Railway Association which is still hoping to raise funds to re-instate the track between Redmire and Garsdale.

After leaving the Moorcock Inn, we decided to explore the nearby Garsdale Head station and its neighbouring cottages. Just beyond the Dandry Mire viaduct (also sometimes known as the Moorcock viaduct due to its proximity to the inn) is a row of railway cottages. These were built by the Midland Railway Company around 1876, the year that the Settle-Carlisle line opened, in addition to the sixteen cottages adjoining the station. Many of these are now holiday lets and would be a lovely place to stay for the marvellous walking in the area, with the added bonus of being able to hop on a train into Leeds on a wet weather day.

There are five passenger trains a day to Carlisle, Settle, Skipton and

Leeds along with plenty of goods traffic – enough to keep signalman Dave Repton busy. 'This is my favourite signal box,' says Dave who is part of the relief team based in Appleby and does regular shifts at Garsdale. 'On a nice day up here, you can't really beat the place. You are in the middle of nowhere and you can see for miles.' The signal box at Garsdale was first built in the nineteenth century but was replaced in 1913. 'All the equipment we use dates back to that time,' says Dave who has been doing the job for twenty years since he left school, and hopes to do it for the rest of his working life. 'The sad thing is that with new technology these boxes may become a thing of the past.'

From the station we drove west to what is known locally as 'The Street' but which has been signposted by the authorities as 'Garsdale'. The reality is, though, that local folk prefer to think of Garsdale as referring to the whole community of some two hundred properties spread over several miles, not just this central row of houses. By the by, The Street might just as well be called The River, since the River Clough and the road run in parallel here, separated only by a wall. The Street Chapel dates back to 1841 and its sign is showing its age in more ways than one. Nearby is a tiny, disused petrol station which suggests that commercial ventures other than farming don't always seem to thrive here.

Towards the end of the row of houses, but on the other side of the road, on a dangerous bend, is a rambling, derelict old property that captures the imagination – we believe it was once called Garsdale Hall. With walls several feet thick and a barn attached, it still has a stately air about it. It has stood in that spot for several centuries and, with a little attention, could stand for several more, so it seems sad that it may just slowly crumble. There might be an opportunity here for someone to save the building and open up a new pub restaurant (though Simon and Caz at The Moorcock won't thank us for the suggestion). On the other hand, perhaps, given the fate of the petrol station, it's not such a good idea. The adjacent church of St John the Baptist is still in use and, unusually in our recent experience, was unlocked. Dating back to 1861 (but built on the site of a medieval church) St John's exemplifies simplicity and cleanliness, though its plasterwork has suffered in recent times from the effects of damp.

Driving on, with milestones regularly announcing how much closer

Dandry Mire
Viaduct

we were to Sedbergh, it felt like we were now in Garsdale proper. The steep valley sides sparkled with rivulets and waterfalls gushing down to the westward flow of the River Clough. The dale appears to be a thriving agricultural area with lots of farms and plenty of sheep and lambs out in the fields. At this point in our journey, certain contrasts were particularly evident: rain and sunshine combined to create overarching rainbows; up on the hill tops of Baugh Fell there was snow, while down in the valley the daffodils were in full bloom.

Our next stop was the viewing point at Langstone Fell. The car park was a potholed and puddled mini Lake District where we saw a pair of extremely shaggy winter-coated ponies on the ground and a military helicopter and jet planes just above us. The vista northwards to the Howgill Fells is worth the trip alone: and, from here, Sedbergh is in clear view though we were not going quite so far. Instead, we embarked on a lovely return journey by taking the Sedgwick Trail Loop Road (named after the famous local geologist) which winds down to the delightful Danny Bridge, where photographers will certainly want to pay their respects; past Hole House Farm, over a ford,

and on towards Lindsey Fold Farm. All along this single track route there are lots of gates to open (and close) which provide the passenger with an interesting intellectual as well as physical challenge – each latch is different and some of the gates are quite heavy, providing a good workout! If you're a solo motorist, you certainly have your work cut out. Coming back down onto the main road, heading eastwards, you pass a picture-perfect cottage called Badger Dub Cottage and an appealing looking B&B, The Old Joinery.

Keep heading eastwards and you return to Hawes, unless you are tempted into Garsdale's offshoot dale, Grisedale, of which more later, or back into the Moorcock Inn for an early tea. As in every dale, there's plenty to discover in Garsdale if you're not simply rushing through: avoid the highways and travel the by-ways!

Garsdale

Fact File

The Moorcock Inn
Garsdale Head, nr Sedbergh,
Cumbria LA10 5PU
☎ 01969 667488.
🖱www.moorcockinn.com
Open every day for lunch and dinner.
Bed and Breakfast accommodation also
available.

Holiday cottage to let
at Garsdale Head station
Nr Sedbergh, Cumbria LA10 5PQ
Cottage number Five,
☎ 0114 269 6008
🖱www.5railwaycottages.co.uk

The Old Joinery Bed and Breakfast
Garsdale, nr Sedbergh,
Cumbria LA10 5PJ
☎ 015396 20309.
🖱www.theoldjoinery.com

The Garsdale, Bed and Breakfast
Garsdale Head, nr Sedbergh,
Cumbria LA10 5PU
☎ 01969 667096.
🖱www.thegarsdale.com

Wensleydale Railway
🖱www.wensleydalerailway.com

79

A lone sheep
stands guard
over Grisedale

THE DALE THAT WILL NEVER SAY DIE
Grisedale (August)

In 1975 Yorkshire Television producer Barry Cockcroft – who two years earlier had 'discovered' Hannah Hauxwell – made a documentary entitled *The Dale that Died*. The film focussed on sixty-one-year old former miner Joe Gibson, originally from the North East, who had begun a new life as a sheep farmer in Grisedale.

This remote Yorkshire valley was once the home to fourteen families but by the mid-1970s Gibson was the only farmer living and working in the dale, though assisted by his wife and son. Theirs was a hard life and the film repeatedly referred to Grisedale as having 'died' in the sense that the small population had moved away from the valley and the deserted houses were slowly becoming derelict. At the end of the film, Joe was left facing the fact that the farm's owner wanted to sell the land and property, in effect putting an end to Joe's dream of handing over the running of the farm to his son. We wanted to find out what was happening in Grisedale now, whether anyone still lived there, why they lived there and what makes it such a special place. So we spent our day in that particular dale speaking to the people who had made the place their home.

On entering Grisedale from Garsdale, the initial impression is of having stumbled upon a secret, semi-wild place that few people really know about. There are buildings dotted about, some derelict but many with obvious signs of life. Today, while the dale could not exactly be described as thriving, it is certainly well and truly 'alive'. The land is farmed by John Pratt who was born and bred in the dale and now lives just outside Grisedale itself in Grouse Hall. The population of Grisedale is still fairly small and its make-up is quite different from fifty years ago. Among the eight residents only one – farm worker Matthew Gibson, grandson of Joe – is involved in working the land for a living. A cul de sac dale bordered by Wild Boar Fell, Grisedale is not the sort of place you pass through on the way to somewhere else: you have to have a reason for going there and that, it seems, is part of its attraction for those who live there.

John Pratt is the only farmer still working in Grisedale. We met John as he rode across a rough field on his quad bike with young farm worker Matthew Gibson. 'All the other farmers have left,' says John. 'We had a couple of hard winters and a lot of people moved out. Today, I'm the only farmer here. I've been here all my life. I have sheep and horses. I breed horses for showing and breeding – black and white heavy cobs and Shetlands. I sell them all over the UK and Europe.' Matthew Gibson, grandson of Joe, lives in the same farm, Mouse Syke, that his grandparents lived in over thirty years ago and works with John on the land every day. Apart from John and Matthew, all the other residents of Grisedale are 'incomers'. What they all have in common, says John, is that 'they fell in love with the valley.'

Ian Squires worked for the Metropolitan police for thirty-two years and he and his wife Joan had been living in Moor Rigg Cottage in Grisedale for eleven years when we met them. Originally from Broadstairs in Kent, they both loved the wildness of their adopted home but were planning to move back to the south to be closer to family. 'You have to want to live here,' says Joan. 'It's not somewhere you would come unless you wanted peace and quiet. It's a beautiful place and more rustic than the rest of the Yorkshire Dales.'

The Squires have no mains water at their cottage – their water supply is from a natural spring – but there is mains electricity. They go food shopping to Hawes or Sedbergh or Kendal once a week for provisions. 'We keep a good store cupboard,' says Joan. 'You've got to because you can't just nip out to get something if you run out.'

The couple used to holiday in the Dales regularly and saw Moor Rigg cottage while trekking through Grisedale. 'We saw this place for sale and so we took the plunge,' says Ian. 'It was quite a major life change. I was working in Victoria in London – Grisedale was quite different! It's a unique place. It grows on you. The light is fantastic, every hour is different and the landscape changes all the time.'

Although Grisedale is very definitely off the beaten track, both Ian and Joan say they never feel isolated. 'There's always something going on,' says Joan. 'We get a lot of walkers and holidaymakers and lots of youngsters doing their Duke of Edinburgh awards; so there are always people around.' Ian agrees: 'There's always something happening up here. Prince Charles comes up to Grisedale once or twice a year to shoot on the grouse moors and stays nearby. Then there was a lot of activity a few years ago when Vince Clarke of Erasure bought a house just down the valley... he didn't stay in the end, though.'

Pat Thynne is a Leadership Development Consultant for Local Government and lives in a restored farmhouse called Reachey (but referred to as 'Reacher' in the book of *The Dale that Died*).

The sunshine breaks through in Grisedale

A Day In A Dale

Pat first saw Grisedale back in 2001. As soon as she saw the derelict house, Reachey – which she has now had restored – she knew that she was going to live there one day. 'I felt like I belonged here. I think the house chose me,' she says. The process of buying the property and gaining planning consent took three years while the old farmhouse remained a ruin. After the formalities were completed, Pat employed a local architect. 'He was great and we worked really well together on the plans,' she says. 'I wanted the main house to be completely traditional.' The results are impressive, combining glass and traditional materials to provide a modern home with a stunning outlook while retaining many of the original building's features.

Bringing Reachey back to life was, for Pat, a labour of love. 'I had great builders, all local guys,' she says. 'In particular, the stonemason, Ernie, was wonderful – an artist with stone. I loved watching him work. It's a shame that those skills are not necessarily being passed on.'

Grisedale's appeal is not for everyone but, to Pat, it is a very special place. 'I love its 'almost wildness'. The silence is wonderful; the darkness is wonderful. Since coming here, I have started watching birds. You also see deer and hares. And there is the occasional walker. It is so peaceful – there are no coach parties!' Less appealing, too, for

A pony feels the Grisedale breeze

some, might be the weather compared with milder climes, but not so for Pat: 'I love the extremes – when the rain is horizontal and there's ice everywhere. It's something about being self-reliant – I like that. The dale floods in a storm, and then I have a mini moat around my house. Grisedale Beck starts to lap at the tyres of my car but the house stays dry.'

Pat's self-reliance does not extend so far as to wish to isolate herself from the rest of humanity. Though she does enjoy being alone for some of the time, she also ensures she gets what she calls 'community therapy' on a regular basis and is very fond of her neighbours. 'I have city friends who ask if I get lonely,' says Pat, 'but I think that solitude is different from loneliness. I would feel far more lonely living alone in London.'

Pat, who is a lawyer by training and now runs her own consultancy business, recognises that she has had to adapt to her new way of life but is grateful for the benefits it has brought: she laughs as she says, 'My friends down South can't conceive of the idea of not having takeaways nearby. You do slow down here. I was in London for work a few weeks ago and I was battling against the flow of commuters trying to get to a meeting. I was getting really angry and I realised that when I lived in London I was like that all the time.' She continues: 'I think there will be an increasing number of people like me running away from the city since it's so grim to live there – and it's increasingly possible to work from home,' even if home is out in the semi-wilds.

Pat often thinks back to the time when Reachey was a farmhouse and byre with no running water or electricity. 'I do feel slightly self-conscious about how much space I have compared to the people who used to live here,' she admits. 'It's recorded that they had twelve children plus a farm worker living in the main house.' Once or twice a year parties of people who used to live and work in Grisedale come back to visit. 'There are a couple of brothers and their mother who I have met,' says Pat. 'They say they really like what I have done with the house, which gives me great satisfaction. The brothers say that it used to take two hours to walk to school from here – and they used to do it every day, even in bad weather.' Pat considers it a privilege to live in Reachey today. 'I'm not moving!' she says, laughing. 'I'm going out of here feet first.'

A Day In A Dale

Mary Robinson lives at Aldershaw, a seventeenth century farmhouse. She moved there from Cheshire eleven years ago with her husband Peter.

Mary is originally from the West Riding of Yorkshire and when she and her husband were looking to move from Cheshire, they started searching for a property in Cumbria. 'While we were house hunting we just happened to turn right off the motorway instead of left. When we saw the house we fell in love with it straight away.'

Mary's husband had already retired so he moved in straight away but Mary was still working at that time as a director for National Children's Homes and would travel up at the weekends. 'It was wonderful coming home off the motorway and approaching the dale,' says Mary. 'And the weather is not as bad as people had told us. One of the magical things about Grisedale is that, on a beautiful day, it's just a little sanctuary.' However, she knows that life would have been very hard for those trying to earn a living from the land. 'I think if I had read the book *The Dale That Died* before coming here, I'm not sure I would have wanted to live here.'

Even for today's residents in Grisedale, there can be some hardships. 'The electricity went off for about a week not long ago,' says Mary. 'I just happened to be in Hawes and I went into the office to ask when the electricity would be back on and they didn't know it was still off in Grisedale! They thought it had been switched back on at the same time as Garsdale. It was a good job I was passing...'

Mary's house was restored in 1986 by a builder based in Cumbria. 'It had been derelict since the 1930s when the family who owned it left,' explains Mary. 'We didn't have to do a tremendous amount when we moved in, just make it comfortable for us.' Sadly, Mary's husband had died a few months before we met her and she was uncertain at that time whether she would stay on alone but admitted that 'it would be very hard to leave.' Her family and friends love the house and the dale as much as she does. 'The best thing about living here is the peace and tranquillity. Everyone who comes to stay says that they feel they have really relaxed and re-energised.'

Mary felt very comfortable with the slow pace of life in Grisedale and the fact that there is time to stop and stare. 'I like watching the seasons and the wildlife. The oystercatchers come back here at exactly

Derelict
buildings scatter
the Grisedale
countryside

A Day In A Dale

**Grisedale residents
Matthew Gibson
and John Pratt**

the same time every year – the first week of March – and you see them teaching their babies to fly.' Although the residents of Grisedale are few and far between, Mary feels that there is a growing sense of community. 'We all look out for one another.'

Sally McMullen owns Fea Fow, a former farmhouse in Grisedale which is currently being renovated. Sally is a piano teacher who lives in Cambridge and comes up to Grisedale every week. She organises her work so that she teaches four days back to back and then spends the remainder of her time in the dale.

When we spoke to Sally she had been living part-time in Grisedale for about five years. Originally she had stayed in Moor Rigg cottage and was lodging with neighbour Pat Thynne at Reachey while the renovation of Fea Fow was being completed. Sally's love of remote places developed through a friend who lived in Long Sleddale, near Kendal. 'I came up to stay in her house a few times and I realised I needed to be in the North. What I love about it is the 'untamedness' of it all and the different pace of life. Cambridge is becoming so crowded and concreted over. There is something about Grisedale – it's secret and you feel a sense of ownership. You get a feeling very quickly that you either belong here or you don't – and I feel a very strong sense of belonging. I would love to live here permanently.'

A poignant aspect of Fea Fow, and a reminder of how different life used to be, is the grave of a small child that Sally found on her land. 'She died during one of the very harsh winters after the Second World War,' says Sally, 'and she was buried under the snowdrops in the garden.'

Tony Roberts and Ian Davidson-Walton were renting East House when we met them. Having sold their accountancy business, they travelled for a while before settling in France. They had moved into Grisedale in December 2007 to be nearer to Tony's elderly parents who live in Leeds.

At first it might seem rather incongruous that two successful businessman, both from the city, could make a life for themselves in one of Yorkshire's remotest dales but it takes no time in their company to appreciate just how contented they are with rural living. In the Dordogne they had lived close to the countryside and knew, when returning to England, that city life was no longer for them. 'When we saw that East House was available,' says Ian, 'we decided to give it a try. We love the peace and quiet: we are not reclusive but it's nice to see people on your own terms.' Even so, they have become firm friends with their neighbours, particularly Pat at Reachey and Mary at Aldershaw.

'Actually you do see quite a lot of people,' says Tony. 'We often get walkers knocking on the door asking where on earth they are!' Ian and Tony rent East House from Linda Fawcett, who now lives in Dent. She was the first person to reoccupy the house after everyone moved out back in the fifties and sixties and she raised her family in Grisedale. 'She said that if we managed to survive the winter, then we could survive anything and we would stay,' says Ian. And she was right, despite some difficulties along the way. 'The first week we were here,' says Tony, 'we lost the water supply – we get water from a spring. It was raining, blowing a gale and pitch black, and Linda came up from Dent to show us what to do. She took me up the fell and cleared the filter out. I've been up there several times since. It was a good initiation.'

A Day In A Dale

'We had to reacclimatise,' acknowledges Ian, 'but I love the sense of seasons here. I have become more and more aware of how the trees and flowers bloom at different times.' When visitors come to stay, Tony tells them simply to listen. 'And you can hear nothing,' he says. 'It's perfectly silent, beautiful.'

Living thirteen hundred feet above sea level an hour and a half's drive from the nearest city doesn't seem to daunt Ian and Tony. Ian is currently writing a book while Tony is following an Open University course. They spend the rest of their time walking, talking, studying – and enjoying the view. 'We have probably become a bit too interested in the weather,' laughs Ian, 'but we do keep up with what's going on in the world.' Tony emphasises just how much they have both fallen in love with Grisedale, its people and its landscape: 'We would like to live here permanently. When I go anywhere else, I can't wait to get back here.'

Grisedale, like many other areas in the Yorkshire Dales, is adapting to new economic realities: over the past hundred years fewer and fewer farmers could attempt to make a living from grazing the uplands. Growing crops is a near impossibility in this terrain and climate, so tending sheep or ponies is the only practical option available. Since families today quite naturally expect a standard of living significantly beyond mere subsistence levels, economies of scale have prevailed, with a farmer now managing two thousand acres or more of grazing land virtually single-handed. That being the case, the restoration of deserted or semi-derelict buildings in Grisedale, re-vitalising them as family homes, weekend retreats, or broadband-friendly eco-workspaces is as good a way as any to ensure the dale's survival. Indeed, far from being the dale that died, Grisedale's future seems to be in safe and sensible hands – this is the dale that will never say die.

The view into
Grisedale - the
indomitable dale

Hardraw Force - a
dramatic feature
of Cotter Dale

THE GROUSE MOOR DALE
Cotter Dale (July)

It's not always possible to choose your weather when fixing a date to spend a day in a dale: so it was that we set out on what felt like the wettest July day in years to explore one of the lesser known of Yorkshire's numerous small dales.

Cotter Dale is a branch line, so to speak, of the western end of Wensleydale, bordering Grisedale and close to Garsdale. As we were driving via Cray and Bishopdale, it soon became clear that water was going play a significant part in the day's events. The Cray Gill waterfall is generally dry in summer but today there was an impressive cascade. At this point it wasn't raining, the sun was hinting at breaking through, but the clouds threatened a continuation of the heavy rains of previous days.

Once in Wensleydale, we headed west, almost but not quite entering Hawes, and crossing the River Ure at Haylands Bridge. A propeller driven aeroplane of World War Two vintage suddenly appeared out of nowhere, thundering very low overhead, filling us with the fear that the aircraft was in danger of plummeting to earth. It didn't. The fisherman standing up to his thighs in the river seemed much less perturbed – he didn't bat an eye. Turning right off Brunt Acres Road you swiftly arrive at the Stone House Hotel. Chris Taplin and his brother-in-law Peter Westwood have been in charge of the hotel since 1991. However, the Stone House has been in the family since 1980 when Chris's parents moved out from Bradford (and the butchering business) to start up a B&B in the Dales.

'They took a bit of a gamble,' says Chris. 'In March 1981 they opened up with four bedrooms on a bed and breakfast basis but they saw that there was potential there. Then the James Herriot books and television series appeared and the tourist trade in the Dales really took off.' The business has been expanded over the years and now there are twenty-four bedrooms and twenty-five staff: although the heyday of the Herriot effect has long since passed, the hotel is still going strong. 'We have loyal regulars who return time and again and the current economic climate might actually work in our favour because people are taking more short breaks closer to home rather than long foreign holidays.' Chris and Peter have also introduced activity breaks, which are very popular, including malt whisky tasting, photography, art and dry stone walling.

Built in 1908 as a gentleman's country residence, the house has an interesting connection with the writer PG Wodehouse who was an acquaintance of the then owner Hugh Crallan. A young and talented cricketer called Percy Jeeves, who worked as a gardener for Crallan, is reputedly the inspiration for the character of Bertie Wooster's butler. A fine cricketer, Percy played for the local team of Hawes and was destined to play for England but, sadly, never got the chance as he was killed at the Battle of the Somme in 1917.

If you turn left out of the hotel car park you quickly come to the left turn to Sedbusk, a quiet and quite beautiful hamlet (prince of the Dales!) perched on a series of ledges to the north of the Ure. There is little through-traffic, but equally there are no shops, no pub, no church: you live or holiday in Sedbusk to escape from most of the trappings of modern life.

Walkers Brian and Sheila Adams are regular visitors to the area from Leicestershire, where the terrain is a little flatter. 'We were both at university in Leeds so we have been coming up to the Dales for holidays for years,' says Sheila. 'It's quiet and it's beautiful – you have the lovely little villages and the wide open moors. It's just so relaxing.' They were taking a well-earned rest on a bench on the small village

Chris Taplin and Peter Westwood at the Stone House Hotel

green. The bench bears a plaque which reads 'On this spot in 1832 nothing happened'. That is the joy of Sedbusk – nothing ever happens here.

In nearby Hardraw, The Green Dragon Inn should be visited for its log fires (even in July), its olde worlde charm, its generous portions of food and its traditional beers. Besides that, in the back garden is the largest single drop waterfall in England, Hardraw Force. For two pounds you can purchase a ticket to walk the quarter mile or so to view the cascade. It is clearly best to see the waterfall after rain and, thanks to the amount of precipitation over the preceding days, what we eventually saw was magnificent and dramatic. We could hear the thundering roar reverberating around the natural amphitheatre of rock long beforehand.

From one waterfall to another: driving west out of Hardraw, and turning right on to the main A684 that links Hawes and Sedburgh, you soon see lay-bys on either side of a bridge. To the right of the bridge is a footpath, accessible to wheelchair users, to Cotter Force. It is certainly worth making the short trip to see these falls. Cotter Force is a very different kind of waterfall from Hardraw. Much broader, but less steep, it resembles a wide staircase, or downwards escalator, hurrying

The beck
flowing through
Cotter Dale

Cotterdale Beck towards its convergence with the River Ure at the bridge.

Around a quarter of a mile beyond Cotter Force is a right turn, signposted to 'Cotterdale only'. Cotterdale is the name of the hamlet about a mile distant, and the valley you enter at this point, rising up,

then dipping down and extending for miles into the distance, is known as Cotter Dale. To your right you are flanked by rising land which forms part of the Pennine Way leading you to Great Shunner Fell which, at seven hundred and sixteen metres, is the highest point for miles around. On the northern horizon is Cotterdale Common – shooting country.

A Day In A Dale

Amongst the fields delineated by a network of dry stone walls and fencing we noticed some cows and a farmer walking off to deal with a mother and calf who had separated themselves from the herd. Despite the inclement weather, Thomas Iveson was happy to chat. Though he doesn't live in the dale, he is the only farmer in Cotter Dale, looking after his small herd of cattle and about six hundred sheep.

'I've been farming here all my life and my father before me,' he said. 'We have land elsewhere too and we have never lived in Cotter Dale – we live in Hawes – but we are the only family farming here now. It can be tough up here in winter and it's very solitary work but that's partly why I like it. I get on well with the gamekeepers who live in Cotterdale though and I see a lot of hikers. Ninety-five per cent of them are great but some of them don't have much country sense: they leave gates open and the sheep get out which is a problem for us. I've been doing this since I was a child – after school and weekends and everything – it's all I've ever known. It's peaceful and you are not bothered by anybody. When you have the whole valley to yourself on a nice day it's great.'

In the hamlet of Cotterdale, most of the cottages, which date from the seventeenth century onwards, are weekend and holiday homes, though there are some permanent residents. The occasional building looks a little neglected, hinting at what nature would do in reasserting its authority were the village to become truly deserted. There were signs advising us of the presence of red squirrels – so we kept an eye out for them and spotted one on a wall later. Discovering that the path through the forest plantation was closed, preventing access eastwards onto the Pennine Way, we retraced our steps into the hamlet and met holidaymakers Brenda Winfield and Rebecca Rogers, regular visitors to Cotterdale, who were staying in the Old Chapel cottage. In the garden were three headstones, reminders of the time when the entire garden was a graveyard.

Thomas Iveson had advised us to look out for the gamekeepers who lived in the village and, sure enough, we found two of them doing maintenance work on their specially-equipped quad bikes. The prettier of the two was Amy Lucas, a twenty-year-old from Kirkby Stephen and one of few women gamekeepers in the country. It's clear that she loves what she does – this is a job for life, she says, 'but I don't really regard it as a job.' Her colleague, head gamekeeper Paul Starsmore, agrees. 'I've been doing this for twenty-two years and, no, it's not a job – it's a way of life.' The appeal of the job is obvious to Amy: she loves working outdoors, although the weather in this part of Yorkshire is not always appealing. 'You have to be used to the rain,' she laughs, 'but when it's sunny up here it's lovely and it makes it all worthwhile.' Standing on the upper reaches of Cotter Dale, you can see for many miles in every direction. When the wind isn't blowing, it's possible to sense the kind of silence that few human beings in this country are ever able to experience. The vast area of moorland that is Amy's domain is made more accessible by Land Rover or quad bike, though walking is still an essential requirement. 'You have to keep your quad bike in good condition because you wouldn't be able to do your job without it,' says Amy. 'I do a lot of walking too. I need the bike to get up to where the traps are but then I have to walk to get them. I think gamekeepers in the past must have been very fit!'

On the drive home, we retraced our route to the monotonous rhythm of the windscreen wipers, with clouds descending lower than the surrounding hillsides. However, the overall conclusion we both drew is that there is no weather that guarantees seeing the Dales at their best. The fact is: the Dales offer up differing joys whatever the weather.

Fact File

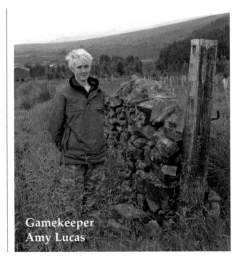

Gamekeeper
Amy Lucas

The Stone House Hotel
Sedbusk, Hawes,
North Yorkshire DL8 3PT
☎ 01969 667571
🖰 www.stonehousehotel.com

Cotterdale Cottage Holidays
☎ 0191 2519366
🖰 www.cotterdale-cottage-holidays.co.uk

The Green Dragon Inn
Hardraw,
North Yorkshire DL8 3LZ
☎ 01969 667392
🖰 www.greendragonhardraw.com

A lane in Wensleydale -
gateway to cheese making!

THE CHEESE-MAKING DALE
Wensleydale (December)

Having reached the end of this particular series of days spent exploring Yorkshire's endlessly fascinating dales, we decided to save the most famous of the dales to last. Deservedly renowned in its own right, Wensleydale is nevertheless now known the world over thanks largely to the cheese-eating habits of an adorable animated cardigan wearer and his world-weary dog, namely Wallace and Gromit. More of which later.

Our day in a dale began by approaching Wensleydale from the east via Ripon and the beautiful riverside village of West Tanfield with its arching, iconic, handsome bridge over the Ure. The land hereabouts is fairly flat and gives little indication of the hillier regions you encounter to the west. Even so, West Tanfield is somewhere to become acquainted with, and not only for the sake of the Marmion Tower, nestling close to the village church of St Nicholas.

This impressive tower, actually a gatehouse, was once the main entrance to a manor house that has long since vanished, but was described in the early sixteenth century by John Leland (Henry VIII's official Antiquarian) as possessing 'a fair tourid (towered) gate and a haule (hall) of squarid stone.' The crenulated Marmion Tower (the name comes from the family name of the original owners of the manor house) was altered several times in the fourteenth century as a result of which the upper rooms were eventually used as domestic chambers. A noticeable feature of the tower from the outside is its large, projecting oriel window on the first floor, looking like a small-scale Juliet balcony. There is a door under the arch of the tower that permits access to the upper floors via a steep and narrow stone staircase. Unfortunately, for today's visitors there is no access to any of the rooms or to the rooftops, so the climb is for exercise only, with no views available. In 1513 the manor house came into the possession of Elizabeth Parr, grandmother of Katherine Parr, the only wife of Henry VIII to survive him.

Another reason to linger here is that the village has two fine pubs, the friendly and welcoming Bull Inn and the Bruce Arms, now run as a partnership between artist David Stead and chef Hugh Carruthers, formely of the Michelin-starred and renowned Yorke Arms at Ramsgill in Nidderdale. It was at the Bruce Arms that well-known fisherman/author Francis 'Max' Walbran was laid out after drowning in the Ure just over a century ago – look out for his distinctive commemorative cross in St Nicholas's churchyard. With two such eating and drinking establishments only a stone's throw apart, a weekend rather than a snatched half hour is needed for the tourist to do justice to what West Tanfield has to offer.

Almost all of our Dales' visits have been to smaller dales which you can see a great deal of in the daylight hours of a single day. Trying to see the whole of Wensleydale in close to the shortest day of the year is well nigh impossible, hence our brief stop in a town where you really need to linger, especially if you are interested in beer and brewing. The smell of Masham on brewing days lures many a tankard-touting tourist to the Theakston's and Black Sheep visitor centres, both of which we have enjoyed thoroughly on previous excursions. Also highly recommended (close to the Black Sheep site) is the pub, restaurant and hotel, The White Bear – a lovely place to wine and dine, or ale and regale, as well as rest your head for the night.

Only as you pass the road sign announcing your entry into Richmondshire do you begin to feel that you are in true dales country, which just about coincides with the Yorkshire Dales National Park notices. At almost exactly this point, you arrive at Jervaulx Abbey which, on a cold winter's day in December, we had entirely to ourselves.

Aysgarth
Upper Falls

Founded in 1156, the Abbey was once a great Cistercian monastery until it was ransacked during the Dissolution of the Monasteries in the 16th century. Today it is an atmospheric ruin – a wonderful, truly magical place with numerous nooks and crannies to explore. Tranquil and elegantly overgrown with wild flowers, ivy and other climbing plants, it is resonant with history – which seems to seep from its crumbling walls. Its massive scale, even as a ruin, is still apparent and extremely impressive. Jervaulx is the second largest privately owned Cistercian monastery in the country and has for the past forty years been in the care of the Burden family. Today the abbey is looked after by Ian and Carol Burden and their two daughters, Gayle and Anna. There is an honesty box for donations towards the Abbey's care and upkeep.

One of Yorkshire's most pleasing villages, East Witton is always a delight to encounter, with its white picket fencing and ageless charm. The lane that runs through the centre of the village green eventually brings you (by means of a very narrow single track) to Coverham and on into Coverdale, but you are well advised to simply stroll along in front of the Georgian cottage terraces which look as though they have just jumped off the pages of a Jane Austen novel. Another reason for

A Day In A Dale

Askrigg still
benefits from
James Herriot-
inspired tourism

stopping here, at least for a coffee if not lunch or dinner, is to call in at the Blue Lion, one of the region's favourite gastropubs and hotels.

We stopped, again very briefly, in Middleham because it's impossible not to want to visit the castle when you are nearby, especially when the sun (of York) breaks through in Richard III's childhood home. We were also interested in visiting a French bistro, The Castle Restaurant, which had been highly recommended to us but we were disappointed to discover has been closed for a little while now. Even so, Middleham is full of good pubs, restaurants and cafes – a great location for basing yourself for a Dales holiday.

While photographing the unusual battlemented bridge close to Middleham, we encountered two fishermen who were abandoning their angling in the Ure due to the extreme cold. Their only hope of a catch might have been frozen fillets. Leyburn is another tourist centre (where we bought sandwiches for a peripatetic picnic). There are plenty of pubs, like The Black Swan, and shops that you won't find on the average high street – such as Wray Bros Ironmongers, the kind of shop (like Mortons in Ilkley) which can sell you almost anything you need for the home or garden, the full

An early winter
morning in
West Tanfield

range of which – including charcoal, curtain rails, barbecues, floor tacks and fancy goods – is advertised on large oval plaques on the outside wall.

Wensley, the small village that gives the dale its name (though some locals still refer to Yoredale, after the river Ure) provides the entrance to Bolton Hall, home of Lord Bolton who recently handed on responsibility for the running of nearby Bolton Castle to his son Tom Orde-Powlett and his wife Katy. The church in Wensley, Holy Trinity, is administered by the Churches Conservation Trust: though it has not been de-consecrated, the building is no longer used for regular services despite its beauty, history and links to the Orde-Powlett family who

have owned Bolton Castle since it was first built over seven hundred years ago.

Some visitors may recognise the church for its role in the television series *All Creatures Great and Small* for it was here that the internal shots for the wedding of James Herriot to his wife Helen were filmed. (The real life Alf Wight was in fact married to his wife Joan in Thirsk in 1941, though they did honeymoon in Wensleydale, staying at The Wheatsheaf in Carperby while also, during the daytime, inoculating cattle!).

Next stop would have been West Witton, famous for its summer festival in which an effigy of the giant Bartle is burnt, but the narrow

107

main street was impossible to park along, and the car park for the renowned Wensleydale Heifer pub and restaurant (a favourite haunt of actor Robert Hardy from his vet series days) was already overflowing. Next time.

At Swinithwaite we parked in a lay-by having glimpsed through the bare winter trees the appealing sight of the Temple Folly behind a tall roadside wall. From here you can enjoy mid-distance views of Bolton Castle (and its charming hamlet of Castle Bolton) on the other side of the Ure. The folly seems currently to be used as a rental holiday home but has enjoyed an interesting history going back more than two hundred years as a hunting lodge and belvedere. Not far from here, if you follow a woodland path south for half a mile, are the remains of an ancient Knights Templar chapel.

At Aysgarth we viewed the impressive and swollen Upper Falls before crossing the river and heading west from the edge of Carperby towards Askrigg. En route we decided to call in at Nappa Hall, a fortified manor house of some distinction which was sold two years ago. Traditionally the home of the Metcalfe family for many centuries, the intriguing house has a history dating back to the late thirteenth

Bolton Castle - as viewed from Swinithwaite

century and, like so many other such surviving structures from an ancient past, has tentative associations with Mary, Queen of Scots – though it's true she was incarcerated nearby at Bolton Castle for several months.

Running a little out of puff, our whistlestop tour next brought us to Askrigg, another location brought to the public notice by the Herriot TV series which enchanted viewers with its appealing portrayal of life in the Dales as it once was lived. The most photographed building in the village is Skeldale House, close to the King's Arms pub and the church. From here, TV vets Christopher Timothy, Robert Hardy and Peter Davison were regularly seen emerging to go on their rounds. Askrigg still benefits from tourism but it is a working village inhabited by real people. It's the home of Askrigg Ale, one of the popular beers brewed by Rob Wiltshire whose microbrewery, the Yorkshire Dales Brewing Company, is located at Seata Barn, up one of the many lanes and ginnels that characterise the village. Along another alleyway near St Oswald's church we found a pottery, run by Andrew Hague for more than thirty years. His back garden is a haven for feeding birds and indeed a haven for anyone seeking quiet and serenity. We much

The view south from the Buttertubs Road

admired his creations, both artistic and practical, bought a beautiful small jug and will definitely visit again.

If you have time, there are lots of walks that start from the village and recommended is the walk to Mill Gill Force and Whitfield Gill Force. Time was against us today – the light was fading fast and still we wanted to get to Hawes before the famous Wensleydale Creamery closed for the day.

Hawes, at the western end of Wensleydale with Great Shunner Fell dominating the view to the north, is a popular town with all who live nearby, particularly farming folk who rely on the livestock market for sales, but also for shopping and socialising. For tourists, also, Hawes has much to offer with hotels, restaurants and cafes, and attractions such as the Creamery, home of Wallace's favourite cheese. Tuesday is

Fact File

Cockett's Hotel
Market Place, Hawes,
North Yorkshire DL8 3RD
☎ 01969 667312
www.cocketts.co.uk

The Dales Countryside Museum
Station Yard, Hawes,
North Yorkshire DL8 3NT
☎ 01969 666210
www.thedales.org.uk

Hawes Ropemakers
W R Outhwaite & Son
Town Foot, Hawes,
North Yorkshire DL8 3NT
☎ 01969 667487
www.ropemakers.co.uk

Penny Garth café
Market Place, Hawes,
North Yorkshire DL8 3RD
☎ 01969 667066
www.pennygarthcafe.co.uk
Popular with motorcyclists, cyclists, walkers

Herriot's Guest House and Gallery
Main Street, Hawes,
North Yorkshire DL8 3QW
☎ 01969 667536
www.herriotsinhawes.co.uk

Andrew Hague,
Askrigg Pottery
Old School House, Askrigg,
North Yorkshire DL8 3HN
☎ 01969 650548
www.thedales.org.uk/AndrewHague

The White Bear Hotel
Wellgarth, Crosshills, Masham,
North Yorkshire HG4 4EN
☎ 01765 689319
www.thewhitebearhotel.co.uk

Yorebridge House hotel
and restaurant
Bainbridge,
North Yorkshire DL8 3EE
☎ 01969 652060
www.yorebridgehouse.co.uk

market day when the town attracts the kind of trade more often associated with weekends at the seaside in the summer season. Hawes is known as the 'little capital' of Wensleydale and Yorkshire's highest market town.

Having been to Jervaulx Abbey earlier in the day, it was apt to discover at the Creamery's small museum that Wensleydale Cheese derives from a recipe created by the French Cistercian monks who settled at Jervaulx in the twelfth century. Though we'd driven in the rough equivalent of a straight line, we felt as if we'd come full circle. A few cheesy purchases – including a large chunk of Jervaulx Blue – ensured that our Grand Day Out (thank you Nick Park and the Creamery's slogan writers) was one that we'd remember for a while to come.

A Day in a Dale

Kings Arms
Market Place, Askrigg, North
Yorkshire DL8 3HQ
☎ 01969 650817

The White Rose Hotel
Main Street, Askrigg,
North Yorkshire DL8 3HG
☎ 01969 650515
🖝www.thewhiterosehotelaskrigg.co.uk

Yorkshire Dales Brewing Company
Seata Barn, Main Street, Askrigg
North Yorkshire, DL8 3HG
☎ 01969 622027
🖝www.yorkshiredalesbrewery.com

**Jervaulx Abbey and Park House
Guest House**
*The ruins of the abbey are open to the
public and are privately owned.*
Jervaulx, Ripon HG4 4PH
☎ 01677 460184
🖝www.jervaulxabbey.com

**Wensleydale Heifer Hotel
and restaurant**
West Witton,
North Yorkshire DL8 4LS
☎ 01969 622322
🖝www.wensleydaleheifer.co.uk

The Blue Lion
Restaurant with rooms
East Witton, Nr Leyburn,
North Yorkshire DL8 4SN
☎ 01969 624273
🖝www.thebluelion.co.uk

The Bull Inn
West Tanfield,
North Yorkshire HG4 5JQ
☎ 01677 470678
🖝www.thebullinnwesttanfield.co.uk

The Bruce Arms
West Tanfield,
North Yorkshire HG4 5JJ
☎ 01677 470325
🖝www.brucearms.co.uk

The waves
roll in at
Semerwater

THE SEMERWATER DALE
Raydale (May)

Raydale didn't quite live up to its billing on the day of our visit – with a name like that we anticipated unbroken sunshine, though the occasional ray of light did break through the low cloud to suggest how magnificent the view would be on an unblemished summer's day. No matter: the sun doesn't shine every day in Yorkshire (you may be surprised to learn) and the mistiness and light drizzle created a special, dramatic atmosphere.

Our approach into this attractive little dale was from the south up through the village of Thoralby into Aysgarth and then taking the road parallel to Wensleydale's main road through the enchanting village of Thornton Rust. Take time to have a look at the intriguing small chapel, Thornton Rust mission, as well as the impressive Hall and the Village Institute, erected in 1924 and bearing a plaque in memory to the men of the village who died in the 1914-18 War, a sober reminder that even such tiny settlements as this were touched by that terrible conflict.

We turned right at the bend in the road at Cubeck, then left onto the main road at Worton. You get a tantalising glimpse of the attractions of Bainbridge only a mile further on; however, we decided to save these for later and instead turned off towards Stalling Busk, entering Raydale proper. From this road you get a good view of the distinctive anvil-shaped peak of Addlebrough, though it's better appreciated from further west. Very quickly you see the meandering River Bain (reputedly the shortest river in England) just as the lake of Semerwater hoves into view. Continuing southwards and upwards, with the lake to your right, you eventually enter the delights of Stalling Busk, a small community of farms, dwellings, an artists' studio, a church and an appealing B&B. First stop was Raydale Preserves, a thriving jam and chutney-making enterprise operating out of School House Farm.

The shop and tea room were set up by Lesley Kettlewell and her husband Derek over thirty years ago. Lesley made us very welcome, giving us advice about what to see in the local area and the viability of certain tracks across the hills. Our conversation was interrupted when several cows sauntered past the open back door and a voice from the kitchen enquired: 'Are your cows meant to be out, Lesley?' The answer was in the affirmative but she still had to excuse herself to go and see to them.

Lesley, the great-granddaughter of Elijah Allen who established the well-known independent grocer's shop in Hawes, is assisted by three workers, one of whom is Lisa Webb. She explained, shortly before being whisked away to 'act as a wall' for returning sheep, that all the cooking, preparation and labelling is done on the premises. 'People make a special trip up here to buy the preserves, but there are also some nice walks that start and finish here that we provide maps and guides for.' You are encouraged to taste, which we did – with relish. The gooseberry and elderflower was irresistible, and we ended up buying seven jars of pickles and conserves.

The village is served by a delightful, if architecturally unusual church, St Matthew's, presided over by its vicar, Ann Chapman. Neatly contained within walls that barely allow the church to breathe, there's a sense here that the land is for rearing cattle and sheep, and not too much of it needs to be consecrated to God – especially since, in this part of the world, it's all God's country anyway.

We drove to the north shore of Semerwater (which can be spelt as one word or two, and often is) where you feel very much as if you were on a seaside beach. Waves drove towards the shore as impressively as if you were at Scarborough, a strange phenomenon that seemed more than simply the effect of the admittedly strong wind. In summer

The Old
School House
in Countersett

months, it's possible to go swimming – we certainly didn't. There's boating and fishing here too, but these activities are regulated by Low Blean Farm from where tickets are available. There are many legends and myths about Semerwater, the most famous of which concerns a village lying beneath the lake after a punitive angel disguised as a beggar flooded the valley, sparing only the old couple who offered him food and shelter. If he'd gone to Raydale Preserves and received the welcome we did, there'd be no lake today!

While at the lakeside, we observed the joyous response of a group of schoolchildren to catamaran-kayaking, or some such activity, operated by Low Mill Outdoor Centre under the highly appropriate name Mobile Adventures. Battling against the wind and current, and having to take low water levels into account to avoid grounding, canoes that had been roped together were inching their way towards the lake amidst the whoops and yells of children having a thoroughly wonderful time.

Temporarily by-passing Countersett, we headed south-west, rising high above the lake before descending towards the small farm-based

An old tractor at Bainbridge

community of Marsett, where holiday cottages and caravan lets are available. Along the way we spotted a day-time owl (presumably of the short-eared variety) bobbing about in the field in a manner suggesting that local mammalian wildlife of a particular size (ie small) was at risk, or it might have been defending its nest. Unusual as this moment was, it was perhaps exceeded by our encounter only a few moments later with a motorway maintenance vehicle. Looking like an angry, palpitating, yellow hippopotamus kicking up a storm, it appeared to be sweeping the dusty, narrow country lane for no reason that either of us could fathom in such a remote location.

Our map appeared to invite us to keep heading south towards Raydale House and the intriguingly-named Cock Robin Cottage but, when road turned to track, we realised that we would have to turn back as we were on private property, a fact confirmed for us by the charming if rather cool-mannered gentleman who enquired politely whether we were lost. The houses looked very attractive and we have since discovered that Raydale House is, in fact, a holiday home that's available to rent every month of the year except for May and June.

Turning back, we were rewarded with better views over Semerwater and towards Addlebrough than we had observed before and we then stopped for a proper look around Countersett. This was our favourite spot of the day – a beautiful little village of weathered stone cottages that blended in with and complemented the natural contours of the landscape. Three of the buildings that attracted our attention were Countersett Hall (a rugged, unpretentious seventeenth century manor house with fascinating mullioned windows), the Old School House (an utterly enchanting cottage built on different levels, ideal for the old schoolchild-at-heart), and the Quaker Meeting House (which dates from 1710, and welcomes Friends for worship on the last Sunday of every month at 10.45am.).

The Meeting House is, however, open to visitors every day and we went in to find out more. The serene simplicity of the building's wood-panelled interior, with sets of wooden benches amicably facing each other, conveyed a sense of peace and calm that stayed with us for the rest of the day, even during the fairly testing circumstances we later had to contend with.

As you head north, down the hill towards Bainbridge, to the left is a signpost indicating Beggarman's Road, the local name for the old Roman Road that eventually leads to the Pennine Way and its junction with the Dales Way close to Cam Houses. In fact, some know this byway as Cam High Road.

We fed and watered in Bainbridge (whose village green is criss-crossed by a variety of minor roads as well as the A684 between Hawes and Aysgarth) at the one, unmissable pub, The Rose and Crown Hotel, which claims a history back to the fifteenth century. Its name is prominent enough on the front of the building but, just in case you missed it, it's there again, bolder than ever, proclaiming its identity to the car park. Inside is where the famous Bainbridge horn is on display which, in former times, was blown at nine o'clock every evening between Shrove Week and the end of September as a signal to lost or weary travellers bound for Bainbridge or thereabouts.

After our pub lunch, we went exploring – the village shop, where we stopped for local maps and energy-supplying fudge, is very friendly – and strolled up to the mound, known as Brough Hill, just east of the village. Though there is little evidence of it now, this is the

The falls at Bainbridge

site of a Roman fort, Virosidum, explaining the proximity of the aforementioned Roman Road. You won't find any remains – in fact it is protected by a simple electric fence – but it's worth climbing up as the views back over the village across to Askrigg (made famous by the TV series *All Creatures Great and Small* for which it was a principal location) and east along Wensleydale are delightful. Opposite the stile which leads to the fort is the bridge which gives the village its name. From here you have picture-postcard views of the River Bain and its falls as it tumbles towards the River Ure.

On the way back we decided to try out a mobile adventure of our own by means of the byway that offers a route directly from Stalling Busk to Kidstones. If you look at a map you can see its appeal for it seems to offer a significant short-cut compared with the normal highways. We had been told by Lesley Kettlewell at Raydale Preserves that the track was passable with a suitable vehicle but that in certain weather conditions they had been called upon to 'dig people out'. It certainly looked like a nice road to stroll along and, indeed, we saw walkers heading in our direction. They were travelling faster than we dared to, the route being so rutted and bumpy, with many deep, menacing puddles. Although there were wonderful views along this by-way, at one point we encountered a series of treacherous, deep rocky steps which almost defeated our really rather rugged vehicle, and our nerve. We certainly wouldn't recommend you try it. Next time we'll be doing it the proper way – on foot.

Fact File

Raydale Preserves
Schoolhouse Farm, Stalling Busk,
North Yorkshire DL8 3DH
☎ 01969 650233
www.raydalepreserves.co.uk

Home Farm Bed and Breakfast
Stalling Busk, nr Bainbridge,
North Yorkshire
☎ 01969 650360

Raydale House
Near Marsett. *For further information and booking enquiries*
☎ 0870 191 7998 or 01282 845052

The Rose and Crown Hotel
Bainbridge,
North Yorkshire DL8 3EE
☎ 01969 650225
www.theprideofwensleydale.co.uk

Low Mill Outdoor Centre
Station Road, Askrigg DL8 3HZ
☎ 01969 650432
www.lowmill.com

Thornton Lodge
Country House accommodation,
Thornton Rust
☎ 01969 663375
www.thorntonlodgenorthyorkshire.co.uk

Aysgarth
Middle
Falls

THE DESERTED DALE
Apedale (January)

On one of the wildest, wettest and windiest days of the year, we set out to investigate Apedale, an intriguingly named small valley between Wensleydale and Swaledale. Though there was little evidence of any apes anywhere in Apedale, it is very definitely grouse country and there is also ample indication of Man's industrial impact upon the landscape in the remains of lead-mining buildings, all now in a derelict condition.

Most probably, the origin of the name 'Apedale' is from the pre-seventh century Old English 'appeldael', meaning 'the valley of the apple trees'. There is little chance of fruit growing here today in such an exposed location; however, the valley sides of much of Apedale have recently been planted with seedling trees so that, in years to come, the landscape will be noticeably different from the heathery moorland wilderness it appears to be today.

With so much winter rain having fallen prior to our visit, we thought we would approach our dale via Aysgarth to see the famous falls in full spate. Arriving from the east, we enjoyed a blast from the past before coming into the village when we spotted an old-fashioned timber AA box (no 442), belonging to an era when cars were still called automobiles. In fact, it dates back to around 1956 and is one of a handful of such boxes – phased out in 2002 and their telephones removed – which have been listed in order to preserve them.

Turning right off the main road in Aysgarth at The Palmer Flatt Hotel and the Wensleydale Farmer Pub, we then took the twisting lane down the hill to the River Ure. We heard the falls before we saw them – the force of the water was thunderous as we passed over the bridge and headed for the car park at the National Park centre.

We viewed the Upper Falls – an amazing, powerful rush of water at once impressive and slightly unnerving – from the banks, taking great care not to go too near the edge with the flow of the river being quite so tempestuous. From there we walked the short distance to the Middle Falls which offer the splendid hillside backdrop of St Andrew's church which has the largest graveyard (four acres) of any church in England. At the falls the water was cascading so ferociously and with such velocity that the Ure seemed more like a mini Niagara.

From Aysgarth, our next stopping point was Carperby, a delightful ribbon of village with almost every house or building a history lesson in itself – there's a Quaker meeting house dating back to 1864, a lovely old school building (now a private residence), a Wesleyan chapel and a Market Cross. An obvious port of call in Carperby is The Wheatsheaf Inn, renowned as the honeymoon hotel for Alf Wight and his wife Joan (better known as Mr and Mrs James Herriot). One point of intrigue is that the plaque by the front entrance informs us that the couple married in 1941, two years later than the date suggested in the vet stories. Inside, the oak-panelled residents' lounge has a huge open fireplace and plenty of items of interest hanging on the wall, including a letter from James Herriot to his parents telling them about his marriage. Apparently, Greta Garbo also stayed at the Wheatsheaf in early 1942 during a break from a series of performances at nearby Catterick Garrison.

A little beyond Carperby, heading east, is the turn off for Castle Bolton (the village) which is protected by Bolton Castle (the castle). Just as you approach the castle from below, as we did, you pass under a tree leaning out over the road at an impossible angle. The castle itself is an impressive and imposing edifice that one can normally see for miles around – you get a wonderful view of it from as far away as the head of Bishopdale – but on this visit it was almost camouflaged into the landscape by the gloominess of the weather. The moist mistiness did, however, add an atmospheric air of mystery.

As we walked through the gates, we were approached by a friendly young man pushing a wheelbarrow who informed us that the castle was, in fact, closed from November until March as cleaning and restoration were underway. We asked if we could take some photographs, explaining what we were doing, and he then very kindly offered to give us a tour of the castle. Robert, it turned out, was from Sopot ('it's on the coast, a bit like Whitby in the summer time') near Gdansk in Poland and had been working at the castle after a chance encounter, while he was working as a barman at the Foresters Arms in Carlton in Coverdale, with Tom Orde-Powlett, eldest son of the current Lord Bolton.

Robert has qualifications in silversmithing, blacksmithing and ancient building restoration and is happy to help restore the castle to somewhere near its former glory. 'We are covering areas with gravel; replacing old steps; basically keeping everything as safe and clean as possible,' he explained. 'We need to remove weeds from the walls and bird droppings, both of which do a lot of damage.' The birds also cause other problems. Robert indicated one of the towers. 'That tower is about fifteen metres tall and ten metres of it is blocked with jackdaw nests – they can build those nests in a month.'

Most of the maintenance work at the castle is done by Tom, helped by Robert. 'I was really lucky to meet Robert,' says Tom. 'My fiancée Katie and I had gone out for a meal at the Foresters Arms. Robert was behind the bar and we got talking. I asked him if he would like to come up to the castle to have a look around and he started to come up every day to help out; he was really enthusiastic and very informative.' After a few weeks, Tom offered him a job at the castle and he has been there ever since.

Strictly speaking, the castle is no longer the family home – it was until 1647, but after the castle had been partially ruined by Cromwell during the Civil War, nearby Bolton Hall was built. As a child Tom spent a lot of time at the castle, growing up around what must be one of the best playgrounds imaginable. 'My dad spent 20 years looking after the castle,' he says, 'so from the age of about seven, I was here quite a lot. It was a really great place to be able to play in.' Tom admits that the family's long connection with the castle does create a sense of responsibility. 'It makes you want to do the best you possibly can for the place,' he says. 'But the castle can have that effect on people who don't have that family connection – Robert wants to spend his life here restoring it, so it is a very special place.'

Between them, Tom and Robert have significantly spruced up the castle, including the apartments which once provided accommodation to Mary Queen of Scots and her servants when she was held here under Queen Elizabeth's orders during the year 1568. Work has also been carried out on laying down gravel, improving pavement slabs and clearing away a variety of debris which can accumulate when certain areas of the castle are open to the elements.

The castle has been in the same family since it was built in the late fourteenth century. 'The castle took twenty years to complete,' says Robert during our fascinating and extremely informative tour. 'It was started in 1379 and finished in 1399. It was very modern for its time and in its heyday there were up to two hundred people living and working here.' Since it is privately owned, everything the castle earns from visitors goes back into the maintenance budget and there are plans for extra activities to entertain visitors with each new season.

The adjoining village of Castle Bolton largely exists because of the stone blocks that became available after Cromwell's siege of the castle during the Civil War and its partial destruction by bombardment. (In fact, most of the real damage to the walls was caused a hundred years later by a storm). Robert quipped that, with all the restoration work going on, Lord Bolton might write to the villagers asking if he could have his stone back. The village, though, is a delight and it's easy to see why the BBC did so much filming here as part of the *All Creatures Great and Small* TV series back in the seventies and eighties. It was, of course, on the battlements of Bolton Castle that Alf Wight asked Joan (or James asked Helen) to be his wife.

Leaving the village on a narrow lane to the east, in the direction of Redmire, we crossed the fast flowing stream we had come in search of – Apedale Beck. The track running parallel with the beck is on private land so we turned left onto Hargill Lane, heading uphill in the direction of Grinton. The road runs parallel with Black Hill which walkers ascend when climbing up towards Apedale from Castle Bolton

Bolton
Castle

and on into Swaledale. At the sheep grid we turned left onto the bridleway which becomes Apedale Road.

The fact of its existence originally owes a great deal to the now disused lead mines but today it also services grouse shooting as well as providing a safe, if rugged, pathway for walkers. It was clear to us that with shake holes and ancient mine shafts in abundance, anyone travelling on foot, or on horseback, would be well advised never to stray from the bridleway.

We did actually brave getting out of the car to walk part of the way – though conditions were bracingly elemental, to say the least. As we trudged through the wind and rain, we promised ourselves we would return in summer to walk the path all the way to Apedale Head, a high-level route which, weather permitting, would afford glorious views for miles in every direction.

Apedale Beck flows gently and meanderingly along its uplands course, but more ferociously (at least on this day) as it plunges steeply towards the west of the village of Redmire, joining the River Ure close to Redmire Force (another location, besides Aysgarth Falls, that was

Terrano in
Apedale

used in the shooting of the 1991 Kevin Costner film *Robin Hood, Prince of Thieves*).

Like the beck, we decided now to head down towards Redmire, stopping briefly to visit the railway station. Signs there invite you to call in at the Bolton Arms where you are given a very hospitable welcome by the landlord, John Berry. The pub (used in Herriot filming) is at least twice the size on the inside as it appears from the car park. Then again, the welcome there is at least twice as warm as you would find in many places. John and his wife Pam have been at the Bolton Arms for several years, having moved up from Devon. 'It's fabulous living here,' says John, who is originally from the North East. 'The old

Yorkshire people who live around here are great; they tell you all the stories about what they used to do. That's what I love about being in the Dales, getting to know the people.'

Our return home was an adventure in itself. The day had enjoyed a watery theme – the rain, the falls and the becks – and the way back was a constant and wet reminder of that fact. The roads through Bishopdale and Wharfedale were more like rivers; it wasn't always very obvious how to distinguish between carriageway and watercourse. Despite knowing this area quite well, we had never seen the flow of water impose itself quite so dramatically on the surrounding terrain ever before – so you might just want to check the weather forecast for potential deluges before planning your own adventures in Apedale, or, indeed, anywhere in the Dales where water flows.

Fact File

A Day in a Dale

Aysgarth Falls – *there is a fee for parking at the National Park centre or you can park at the café, for a fee, at the top of the hill in the village.*

Bolton Castle
Castle Bolton, nr Leyburn,
North Yorkshrie DL8 4ET
☎ 01969 623981
✆www.boltoncastle.co.uk
The castle is open to visitors from March until October. Events are organised, school parties are welcome and the castle is licensed for civil wedding ceremonies and other functions.

The Wheatsheaf Hotel
Restaurant and Bar,
Carperby,
North Yorkshire
☎ 01969 663216
✆www.wheatsheafinwensleydale.co.uk

The Bolton Arms
Redmire, nr Leyburn,
North Yorkshire, DL8 4EA
☎ 01969 624336
✆www.bolton-arms.com
Meals and bed and breakfast accommodation.

WHARFEDALE AND NEIGHBOURS

Langstrothdale, Sleddale, Bishopdale, Upper Wharfedale, Coverdale, Littondale

A sunny day at
Beckermonds

THE LONG DALE
Langstrothdale (June)

There will be some who will not be best pleased to be reading this chapter about one of Yorkshire's loveliest dales simply because it's a treasure they would rather remained hidden from popular gaze. They would have a point, too, because Langstrothdale, the fount of the Wharfe, is never more lovely than when you have it all to yourself.

Much of Langstrothdale forms arguably the most attractive leg of the Dales Way, while short distance walkers will be rewarded for their efforts in following the upper reaches of the Wharfe before also perhaps branching off to explore the path alongside Oughtershaw Beck. The road through the dale is very narrow in places but, fortunately, except on holiday weekends, the car-driving tourist is unlikely to encounter much in the way of traffic.

As fine a starting point as any to explore what was formerly a forest hunting ground is Buckden, at the northern end of Wharfedale, famous for The Buck Inn and for the walks up to Buckden Pike. You could spend an age based here, lodging at the Inn, at one of the numerous bed and breakfast establishments, or staying in one of the many holiday cottages. Or do as we did and simply visit for the day.

You are spoilt for choice for tearooms but you would be well advised to pop into the Village Stores to meet Gordon and John, who also run the tearoom in a single-storey building to the rear where you are advised to 'Eat where the locals eat'. Apart from being a partial shrine to the memory of Princess Di, the little restaurant displays a signed authentic *Calendar Girls* picture and cards and letters from grateful customers from as far afield as Australia and the United States. It's also worth seeking out the West Winds tearoom with its lovely cottage front garden, tucked away behind The Buck Inn.

The moment you leave Buckden, you are leaving Wharfedale and entering the 'long valley', which is the literal meaning of Langstrothdale. It won't be long, by car or on foot, before you reach the hamlet of Hubberholme, though some locals still keep alive the name of what was once its adjoining community, Kirk Gill, now ignored by the authorities and retained only in the name of its manor and the moor to the south. There are at least two very good reasons for stopping here – the pub and the church.

The George Inn at Hubberholme has a well-documented history as the location of the centuries-old Hubberholme Parliament. This is held on the first Monday of every year ostensibly for the purpose of leasing church-owned pastureland by auction but (since there has been no change of lessee in years) the event has become more a sociable excuse for a local farmers' beer fest. The present landlord, Barry Roberts, (who used a more colourful expression than 'beer fest') has been there for several years, having previously lived in Doncaster. He first came, he claims, because of 'a fit of madness' – a condition which still happily prevails. The parlour of the pub (the House of Commons) thoroughly deserves the name of snug, and sports examples of trout which have been stranded between Buckden and Hubberholme en route to being stuffed and mounted. There cannot be many locations where one would be more contentedly stranded, unless, of course, you happened to be a trout. The more spacious dining-room, just round the corner, serves as the House of Lords. Though closed as a pub in the afternoons from three o'clock until six, The George offers very comfortable accommodation and is an ideal base for walkers.

The church, dedicated to St Michael and All Angels, boasts one of only two rood lofts in the whole of Yorkshire, protected from the ravages of the Reformation by the church's isolated location. More significantly, to those of a literary bent, the graveyard contains the

Langstrothdale
from above
Buckden

buried ashes of Bradford-born writer and dramatist J B Priestley. A plaque inside the church informs us that 'He loved the Dales and found Hubberholme one of the smallest and pleasantest places in the world.' He was a good judge as well as writer, if given to understatement. The church was originally a forest chapel of St Oswald and nestles neatly into the landscape, surrounded by trees and bordered by an arching bridge and the babbling of the Wharfe's waters over ever-shifting pebbles.

The sharp-eyed should look out for a Bronze Age stone circle beyond Yockenthwaite, a tiny community of houses based around a single farm, and before Deepdale. The circle is visible from the roadside in pastureland adjoining the river beyond a dry stone wall and is made up of twenty-four boulders, with smaller stones placed in between. Some have conjectured it may be the remains of a burial cairn, or part of a walled enclosure. Whatever, it's an intriguing reminder of Man's enduring efforts to leave his mark behind throughout the echoing vaults of history in the world's most beautiful places.

Yockenthwaite Farm, run by Stuart and Elizabeth Hird, is a lovely

Hubberholme
church yard

spot to stay for sensibly-priced bed and breakfast, but it is also the location for the thriving 'Lamb Direct' enterprise which delivers fresh Yorkshire lamb to customers throughout the country by mail order. It's a clear indication of how desirable a spot this is that the farm has been in the same family's continuous ownership for more than a hundred and sixty years.

Beyond Yockenthwaite is a picnicker's paradise. The cracked pavement-like limestone banks of the infant Wharfe, lined by grassy verges, provide rock pools and mini-waterfalls a-plenty. This stretch of the river and road passes through Deepdale, with its green painted iron girder bridge and 1679 Grade II listed farmhouse, West Deepdale Farm, which, like so many of the working farms in this area, offers overnight accommodation.

The natural beauty of this landscape does not diminish the further you progress, so it is no surprise that as you reach Beckermonds you appreciate that this particular collection of houses is not only a farm but also a community of very attractive holiday cottages. If there were tea rooms here they would do very good business in the holiday season, especially as this is about the mid-way point for Dales Way walkers en route between Buckden and the Ribblehead Viaduct. The particular appeal of Beckermonds is that this is where the Wharfe (known as Oughtershaw Beck a little to the north) conjoins with Green Field Beck, and close to where Dales Way walkers heading east first encounter the Wharfe. The arched stone road bridge over the beck and the walkers' wooden footbridge over the Wharfe help make this waterfork a photographer's dream.

A dead tree at Oughtershaw

You could choose to continue west at this point, but drivers need to be advised that you (or your companion) will have to get out frequently to open and close gates and it is not possible to drive any further than to Low Green Field, a country house where a sign on the gate advises 'The black stuff is the road, The green stuff is my grass. Harry'. Make of that what you will. Walkers can continue on their way, joining up with the Pennine Way to the north of Horton-in-Ribblesdale. Drivers will have to turn back, but you will be rewarded with

The George at Hubberholme

wonderful views eastwards along Langstrothdale towards Buckden Pike, though the scenery here suffers the artifice of conifer plantations both to the north and south.

Heading north from Beckermonds, properly speaking you leave Langstrothdale Chase behind and enter upon Oughtershaw Moss, before climbing steeply up Oughtershaw Side and on towards the descent into Sleddale, leading to Gayle and Hawes. At the highest point of this road, your eye will be drawn towards magnificent views of Ingleborough's peak to the west. Oughtershaw (pronounced 'outer shaw' we were informed by the affable London-born farmer we encountered mending his walls) is home to an architecturally appealing semi-derelict chapel. On the edge of the hamlet is a cross erected to commemorate Queen Victoria's Golden Jubilee in 1887.

The Dales Way heads off westwards from Oughtershaw for walkers: drivers might want to turn back at this point to return towards Buckden; alternatively, it's certainly worth making a virtue of journeying the extra miles northwards to see the beck cascade through the village of Gayle, in which case you should refer to our Sleddale chapter.

You emerge into Wensleydale at Hawes, extremely busy on the day of our visit, perhaps part of the reason why Langstrothdale, which we had almost all to ourselves, holds such a special place in the memory.

Fact File

West Winds Yorkshire Tearooms
(and bed and breakfast)
Buckden,
North Yorkshire
BD23 5JA
☎ 01756 760883
www.westwindsinyorkshire.co.uk

Stuart and Elizabeth Hird
Yockenthwaite Farm,
Buckden,
North Yorkshire
BD23 5JH
Tel 01756 760835
www.yockenthwaitefarm.co.uk

The George Inn
Hubberholme,
North Yorkshire, BD23 5JE
☎ 01756 760223
www.thegeorge-inn.co.uk

The Buck Inn
Buckden, North Yorkshire BD23 5JA
☎ 01756 760 228
www.thebuckinnbuckden.co.uk

Low Raisgill Cottage
Bed and Breakfast, Raisgill, Buckden,
North Yorkshire BD23 5JQ
☎ 01756 760351

A Sleddale
cloud descends

THE MISTY DALE
Sleddale (July)

Those who drive regularly on the beautiful road out of Langstrothdale through Oughtershaw and then up, up and dizzyingly up, will know that what greets you at the top can be as unpredictable as mountainous, moorside weather – and weather is, of course, the reason.

Even when the sun is shining to the south, there is the possibility of encountering that intriguing feature of school geography lessons, temperature inversion, which creates clinging clouds of mist on the valley floor. On a couple of occasions when we have headed towards Hawes, our view down Sleddale towards Wensleydale has been rendered surreal by the sea of cloud which has engulfed the world below. If, however, it is clear, and no clouds have fallen out of the sky, the view south-west towards Ingleborough is worth the trip alone.

Up here, with curlews mewing and sheep who claim the road as their own (tyres painted with 'Beware Sheep' adorn the roadside), you feel both metaphorically and literally at a crossroads. You are almost – but not quite – in the wilds here, for civilisation is close at hand. You feel a powerful sense of the past, with a Roman road (Cam High Road) bisecting the modern thoroughfare and offering a splendid walking route most of the way to Bainbridge, site of a Roman fort – yet modern life is inescapable in the form of motor vehicles labouring uphill, and jet fighters tearing through the sky.

Down in the dale, following the line of Duerley Beck, there are farms that have existed for centuries living alongside nearby tourist attractions – particularly in Hawes, home of the world-famous Wensleydale Creamery as well as the Dales Countryside Museum – catering for the modern age of leisure and relative affluence.

There is a Sleddale in Cumbria, there is a Great Sleddale (or Sled Dale) to the north of Great Shunner Fell, but this particular Sleddale is more often referred to as Duerley by those who live here, the name of both the beck and the nearby pastures. Higher up, the waters are joined by Little Ing Gill: lower down, as you approach civilisation, the name changes to Gayle Beck just in time to power the turbines of the recently-restored Gayle Mill, more of which later.

Sleddale is not for the kind of tourist who expects to be pandered to. In fact, Sleddale is really only for those who have a deep love of the countryside and how the countryside is managed by those who make their living there. When we descended into the mists – which were soon to clear – we saw our main task of the day as becoming acquainted with at least some of the people whose hard-fought livelihoods depend upon the livestock that so prettily punctuate the fields and upper moorland for the car tourist.

At West Duerley Farm in the valley, we met friendly farmer's wife Yvonne Bell who has lived at the farm in Sleddale (or 'Sleddle' as she pronounced it) since 1982. Having moved to Yorkshire from Lincoln with her parents when she was just fifteen, Yvonne has been resident in the county for nearly sixty years. 'So I think I am more or less accepted as a local now,' she laughs. She married into a farming family – her husband Maurice has lived in the area all his life – and brought up six children. Before moving to West Duerley, the Bells had lived and farmed in Hawes, with Yvonne running a bed and breakfast from their house. 'Part of the reason we moved here was that my husband didn't ever really like living in town and also our youngest son wanted to farm.' Their son, Stephen, along with his wife and their two children, live in the main farmhouse next door to Yvonne and Maurice's stone cottage.

'The best thing about living here is the quiet,' says Yvonne. 'We are

Gayle Mill
stands proud

not isolated, as such, because we can see the traffic going by on the top road, but it's the peace and quiet that I love. The nearest person to us is a mile away, so you get the best of both worlds. Although I wouldn't want to be without my telephone or my television, I wouldn't like to live anywhere else.' The Bells farm sheep – Leicesters which they breed

Gayle Falls

with Swaledales to create 'mule lambs'. The farming economy being what it is, however, Stephen also has a job with Network Rail; Yvonne explains that many farmers now have to take on another job in order to survive.

Yvonne loves the valley and sees no reason to leave. 'We never go out, really, but we don't get lonely because people always come to visit,' she says. 'And we have never had a holiday; years ago we went to Derby to stay with some relatives of mine for two days and my husband said that was enough for him!'

Maurice, when he appears, is quite a character who is thoroughly immersed in local life. The Bells hold an annual open day in May which is like a mini-country show with rare breed classes, children's races and dog competitions. 'I've lived around here all my life,' says Maurice. His parents used to farm just over the hill in Snaizeholme until they sold the property and land to forester and conservationist Hugh Kemp whom we met in connection with his involvement in the setting up of the Red Squirrel Reserve in Widdale. 'Sleddale is a beautiful valley – very natural,' says Maurice. 'I don't see the point in going away. Why go away when there's so much around here? When you're out on the top of Wensleydale, it's beautiful and on a clear day you can see for miles.' Maurice has worked hard as a farmer all his life and still helps his son Stephen out with the sheep. Before we leave, he entertains us with an ironic reminiscence: 'I could have been a professional footballer rather than a farmer – I played for Hawes and Darlington when I was a lad – but my dad said: "There's no money in football".'

A refreshingly straight-talker, Maurice happily acknowledges he holds contentious views on a number of issues – one such is nearby Gayle Mill, made famous through the BBC's *Restoration* series. A substantial amount of money was spent on the renovation of the mill, money which, in Maurice's opinion, could have been better spent on youth projects in the local community or on affordable housing. We decided that we should go and take a look at the mill for ourselves.

But first we went a little to the north (that is, downhill) of West Shaw farm, where the road is known as Beggarman's Road. Here is a public footpath over a drystone wall and across, on this occasion, a

A Sleddale view

newly-mown field towards Duerley Beck. Already, you can hear the distinctive sound of water tumbling and echoing, though muffled by surrounding trees. By crossing a railed plank bridge and heading north, you follow a footpath alongside the beck which eventually will come out in Gayle but which more immediately leads you to Aysgill Force. When the trees are in leaf, it is very difficult to gain a clear view of these dramatic, plunging falls: no photograph can quite do justice to their majesty in this unexpected setting. We viewed the falls from both sides of the beck and from directly above, all three locations being potentially quite dangerous because of the height and sheerness of the drop. With care and with cunning, there is a means of climbing down to the beckside below the falls – any photographer will be rewarded with spectacular shots – but we are saving such adventure for another occasion.

Driving on into the village of Gayle, we now made a point of stopping off at Gayle Mill. A splendid old Grade II* listed cotton mill, it was one of the stars of the 2004 TV series *Restoration*, presented by Griff Rhys Jones. At the time, the building was on the brink of dereliction but through the programme the mill gained nationwide

Aysgill
Force

recognition for its special place in Britain's industrial and social heritage. This enabled the owners of the mill, the North of England Civic Trust, to secure dedicated funding for a major restoration and conservation project; the mill opened to the public at Easter time in 2008. Mike Thomson, one of the trustees who also leads tours around the mill, told us about its fascinating past. 'It was built in 1784 as a cotton spinning mill and then it had a chequered history until the 1840s. In 1879 they put in the first turbine which was to drive a saw mill and all the joinery machinery and then at the turn of the nineteenth and twentieth century they started producing electricity here.'

In 1925 a second turbine was installed and in 2006 a third one was put in; interestingly, all three turbines were made by the same family-run Cumbrian company, Gilkes of Kendal. All the Victorian engineering and waterpower systems have now been brought back to full working order and the 1879 Williamson turbine is said to be the oldest in situ working turbine in the world. 'One of our directors, Tony Routh, is descended from the people who originally built the mill,' says Mike. 'He has done a lot of work promoting the mill – and Griff Rhys Jones came back up here recently for the programme *Restoration Revisited* to see how we were getting on.'

On a trip to the lovely valley of Sleddale, the visitor can walk through picturesque natural surroundings, seek out some spectacular waterfalls or enjoy a tour of a fascinating historical monument – and all this within a few miles of Hawes, Yorkshire's highest market town and the 'little capital of Upper Wensleydale'. Do call in at the tourist information centre – the staff there are extremely helpful and friendly.

Fact File

Gayle Mill
Mill Lane, Gayle, Hawes DL8 3RZ
☎ 01969 667320
www.gaylemill.org.uk

The Wensleydale Creamery
Gayle Lane, Hawes DL8 3RN
☎ 01969 667664
www.wensleydale.co.uk

The Dales Countryside Museum
Hawes Station Yard, Hawes
DL8 3NT
☎ 01969 666210
www.yorkshiredales.org.uk

New glories -
Bishopdale

THE INSPIRING DALE
Bishopdale (June)

Bishopdale begins where the glories of Upper Wharfedale end. As you drive north in the wet season (which can be pretty much every season in Yorkshire these days) through Cray, you will be greeted by cascading waterfalls aplenty. On the day of our drive – one of uninterrupted warm June sunshine – even Cray Gill could barely manage a trickle alongside the inviting White Lion Inn. You might want to stop in here because the next substantial hint of habitation along the B6160 is the Street Head Inn several miles ahead at the edge of Newbiggin.

In winter, this winding road up to Bishopdale Head can be as treacherous as alpine switchbacks, even after the lightest snowfall. Today it was as gentle as a snow leopard's kitten. Opposite Bishopdale Head, the eye will be attracted west to the view of Kidstones Scar dominating the skyline. Cows graze here, but it is an otherwise lonely landscape. For the early part of this drive, your only company (other than fellow passengers) will be the dale's beck on your right. Whilst still relatively high up, look north for spectacular views of Bolton Castle in Wensleydale – it's a most impressive vista. Beyond the bridge at Ribba Hall, the beck is on one's left and will remain so for the rest of the journey.

Kidstones Scar

The relative flatness of the terrain either side of the beck, in contrast to the steepness of the parallel slopes, tells you that Bishopdale exists because of glacial erosion. The beck itself is too narrow, particularly in the early part of its course, to have caused much erosion on its own. The valley widens out as you approach Newbiggin, beyond which we turned off the road into Thoralby, a delightful village that all too many drivers would ignore as off the beaten track, or only use as a cut-through to Aysgarth. However, you need to take care on the sharp bends on entering the village: the narrowness of the roads is the village's most obvious protection from inconsiderate drivers.

The George Inn at Thoralby dates back to 1732, has accommodation and is a good base for exploring the Yorkshire Dales further. Thoralby is easy on the eye and genuinely tranquil. You could be very happy renting a holiday home here with so much good walking terrain to investigate on the doorstep. South and west, there are hikes to Aysgarth Moor or higher to Thoralby Common with views to Semerwater. Aysgarth Falls and the enchanting cul-de sac village of West Burton are within easy walking reach.

A view of Walden

Returning to the main road, we drove the tiny distance east and north to our main destination for the day. On arrival at West Burton, you can hardly believe quite how lovely it is. For a first-time and, indeed, returning visitor, it really is just breathtakingly beautiful. Photographs don't quite do it justice – its appeal somehow eludes capture – so there is no alternative but to visit it yourself.

The long string of individually distinct cottages (one is actually crenulated) that line up either side of the expanse of village green suggests a cosy, thriving community, as do the butcher's shop, post office, its inviting pub, the Fox and Hounds, and the children's play area. This is a real village not just another settlement made up almost exclusively of holiday homes – of which there are, sadly, now so many in the Dales.

Standing on the village green one experiences a sense of peace and contentment. This really is away from it all; far from the crowd, whether madding, maddening or just plain mad. It is the kind of place where you could imagine sitting for an hour or so simply to stop and stare. Or it could move you to some artistic endeavour. Indeed, Turner

149

A Day In A Dale

The
Bishopdale
vista

was thus inspired, having painted the waterfall (known as Cauldron Falls) at West Burton.

The day we visited, a few amateur artists were similarly engaged. One lady sketching the falls explained that she now lived in Shaftesbury in Dorset, having moved there twenty-five years earlier with her husband's job, but was originally from Richmond in North Yorkshire and came back to visit the Dales every year. 'It's nice in Dorset, but compared to this…' – she gestured at the surrounding stunning scenery and shrugged – '…it's not the same.'

From here we drove up the narrow track towards Walden, just to take a look back along the valley that rises up from the tree-lined Walden Beck and savour the heart-stopping view. It's nicer to walk if you have the time, the inclination and the walking boots. Time is the most important of these since, in this part of the world, you really shouldn't rush anything.

It's almost compulsory when exploring the lesser-known dales to discover where exactly a stream such as Bishopdale Beck joins with its more famous and larger watercourse, in this case the River Ure. As we drove north from West Burton towards Hestholme, close to the meeting of the water ways, we

An artist sketches
Cauldron Falls at
West Burton

saw on our right hand-side a most intriguing sight – what looked like
large stone versions of a Dan Dare rocket and a pepper pot. This is the
grounds of Sorrelsykes Park Hall and these unusual follies date back to
the first half of the nineteenth century. Almost nothing more is known
about them. If you wish to explore on foot, you might discover another
surviving folly, a small arch located on the edge of a rocky outcrop.
There used to be yet another folly in the grounds, the facade of a mock
gothic chapel, but it collapsed after a storm in 1992.

There are further treasures to be uncovered on foot. For example, a
little to the east of Hestholme and close to the village of Swinithwaite
are the remains of a Knights Templar Chapel. There's not a great deal
to be seen now except for a number of intriguing graves but, if you're
like us, you'll want to know more. The military-religious Order of the
Knights Templar, of which so much is made in Dan Brown's *The Da
Vinci Code*, was founded in the twelfth century to protect pilgrims
travelling to and from the Holy Land. Introduced into Britain in 1146,
the Order acquired land throughout the country, including in the lee of
Penhill to build a chapel. The story of the Templars' subsequent

persecution and abolition is fascinating and well worth looking into. It can't be long before Hollywood makes the movie.

Though we were now, in effect, in Wensleydale, we were far too close to the famous Aysgarth Falls to call a halt to our trip just yet. We started with the falls at Cray, delighted in the Cauldron Falls at West Burton – but the best had been saved until last, for the Aysgarth Falls are truly some of Yorkshire's greatest natural treasures and a sumptuous feast for the eyes. You have to park (use the Aysgarth Falls National Park Centre), for the river views can really only be appreciated by following the partly-wooded paths that link the Upper, Middle and Lower Falls. It's not the height of the falls that make them so appealing – they are in fact a series of broad limestone steps, not particularly dramatic but captivating nonetheless.

So, Bishopdale is the gateway to Wensleydale and its particular delights – but Bishopdale should never be seen simply as a route to somewhere else when there is so much to savour in tracing the path of its beck and its tributaries, and in discovering its taverns, its villages, its walkways and waterfalls.

Fact File

The George Inn
Thoralby, Leyburn,
North Yorkshire DL8 3SU
☎ 01969 663256
🖱www.maxgate.plus.com

The Street Head Inn
Newbiggin, Leyburn,
North Yorkshire DL8 3TE
☎ 01969 663282 or 07815 415160
🖱www.streethead-inn.co.uk

The White Lion Inn
Cray, North Yorkshire BD23 5JB
☎ 01756 760262
🖱www.whitelioncray.com

The Fox and Hounds Inn
West Burton,
North Yorkshire
DL8 4JY
☎ 01969 663111
🖱www.fhinn.co.uk

Temple Farmhouse
Bed & Breakfast, Swinithwaite,
Leyburn,
North Yorkshire
DL8 4UJ
☎ 01969 663246
🖱www.templefarmhouse.co.uk

The Wharfe in
full flow near
Kettlewell

THE MAJESTIC DALE
Upper Wharfedale (November)

The drive from Ilkley to Buckden is a route we have taken many times; so often, in fact, that it might almost seem like commuting. However, the nature of the landscape, and the changing seasons and weather, means that the journey is guaranteed to hold new delights and discoveries every time.

The early morning was bright and still but a strange mist descended as we set out after the promise of clear skies. However, the further north we headed, the bluer the sky became so that, although Burnsall was shrouded in mist, by the time we arrived in Kilnsey it was sunny and clear. A low blanket of mist still clung to the damp fields close to the Wharfe but there was barely a cloud in the brightening sky.

We paused to photograph the hurdle-like dry stone walls to the south of Kettlewell before pressing on to Buckden where we stopped to explore. Buckden is a delightful village and a wonderful place to visit; however, a Monday in November is probably not the ideal time to expect tea rooms in the Dales to be open. Both the West Winds and the Village tea rooms were shut as was the village shop, though it had been open earlier in the morning we were assured by Tim Berry, who moved to the village from Leeds with his wife Gwen over thirteen years ago. They instantly dispelled the notion that incomers are not made welcome in Dales villages, but it helps to be a permanent resident rather than a weekender. Their cottage offers one of the finest views – west towards Langstrothdale – of almost any front garden in Yorkshire. 'As soon as I saw that view, I knew I wanted to buy this place,' says Tim. 'Buckden is a wonderful place to live,' adds Gwen. 'There is always so much going on here. It's a thriving community and everyone looks out for each other.' Gwen is one of the founding members of the Buckden Singers who appeared on television in 2009 in Selina Scott's *In Search of England's Green and Pleasant Land*.

During our conversation Gwen and Tim told us about The Buck Inn, which closed in July 2010. There had been some interest from potential tenants, though, and there were hopes that it would reopen soon. The success of this fine old establishment – not least as a stopover for the many people who walk the Dales Way every year – in the past suggests that, in the right hands, this is a business which should flourish, bringing an important focus once more to the heart of the village for residents and visitors alike.

One of the lessons we have learnt over the years of writing these

Dry stone
Kettlewell walls

pieces is that Dales pubs are often closed on Monday lunchtimes, especially with the onset of winter. It shouldn't, therefore, have been a surprise to discover that the Fox and Hounds in Starbotton wasn't open to offer us an early lunch; however, it gave us a chance to look around and to appreciate just how old some of the cottages are in this tiny settlement. Several of the cottages boast lintels which proclaim their age as early to mid-seventeenth century, around the time of the English Civil War. They seem so solid and substantial they will probably be standing for a few more centuries yet.

Kettlewell was definitely open for business, with all three of its pubs serving lunch as well as a tea room and a café. At that time the village primary school was under threat of closure, an issue we had been alerted to by the mannequins and banner at the approach to the village which provide a silent but impressive protest to the proposals. Since the village is now famous for its summer scarecrow festival, to see appealing straw figures dressed as schoolchildren standing close to the bridge communicating their heartfelt message was both poignant and powerful. It worked; the school has now been saved.

We had a quick sandwich at the Blue Bell Inn in a bar dedicated to the memory of Private William Henry Townson who had been the landlord of the pub at the time of the First World War. He enlisted at Skipton in 1916 as a forty-year-old, joining the 4th Battalion Northumberland Fusiliers. Despite being wounded twice he returned to the front and was taken prisoner during the Somme campaign, dying in Germany exactly one month before the Armistice. It felt particularly apt and moving to read of William's courage so close to the Armistice commemorations.

After lunch and a walk around the village, we popped into Zarina's, a tea room that also stocks *Calendar Girls* merchandise since the owner, Zarina Belk, knows all the original Calendar Girls from Rylstone and Cracoe Women's Institute personally. The link with Kettlewell was established when location filming for the hugely popular movie took place here in 2003, Zarina had a small non-speaking role, and the village has benefited from a boost to its tourist numbers ever since. 'It's had a nice effect; we've had visitors from Europe who have seen the film and come to see us. I've lived in this area nearly all my life and Kettlewell is a very special place; it's a really close-knit community. Talking to visitors you find out that a lot of them came here as children and they come back with their own children.' Pictures on the wall show Zarina with the Calendar Girls when the tea room was re-launched in 2006 and some customers mistakenly assume that she must have been one of the original naked posers – but the likelihood of her baring all in her kitchen is precisely zero, she attests. However, Zarina's sales of calendars and other gifts have raised in excess of thirteen thousand pounds on behalf of Leukaemia and Lymphoma Research.

Partly at Zarina's suggestion, we called in at the garage on the southern edge of the village where we met Mick Wilkinson. The garage has been in the family since Mick's father first set up shop in the 1940s. Mick, along with his older brother Bill, had been responsible for getting the children of Upper Wharfedale to school by bus over a period of over forty years during which time they only failed to get the buses out on three occasions because of impassable snow.

Mick's garage is a film set in its own right, the idiosyncratic interior appearing unchanged in the *Calendar Girls* movie. Mick now concentrates on mechanical repairs and supplying petrol but he modestly reveals a remarkable past when asked if he has lived in Kettlewell all his life. 'Well, yes,' he replies, 'but I have travelled quite a bit because of moto-cross.' In fact, Mick and his brother Bill have been all over the world, having both been British Moto-Cross Champions. Mick still gets the bike out and takes on the imposing slopes and crags of Middlesmoor Pastures outside his forecourt.

Heading south from Grassington towards Burnsall, an interesting choice awaits you at the Linton crossroads: turn left to head down to the bridge and the falls, with the distinctive ancient church a short walk downstream; or turn right for the village green adjacent to Linton Beck, with the Fountaine Inn as a magnet for walkers, diners and quaffers and with the elegance of the early eighteenth century Fountaine Hospital almshouses as a pleasing backdrop. We visited the Inn partly for the warmth of the log fire on a cold day. The Inn is part of a small chain which also includes The Wheatley Arms in Ben Rhydding and the Tempest Arms at Elslack. Food here is locally sourced and the only down side is the notice saying that muddy boots aren't welcome.

The church
at Linton

The green is characterised by views of three bridges, one of which we crossed enabling us to meet Robert Chaney, a sprightly eighty-nine-year-old with a mischievous twinkle in his eye. Despite his age, Robert helps maintain the beautiful presentation of the village and was in the middle of sweeping leaves from the packbridge. 'I retired twenty-eight years ago, but I like to keep busy,' he says. Robert was born in Linton 'just the other side of the Inn' and has lived in Wharfedale most of his life apart from a spell serving with the East Yorkshire regiment overseas during the Second World War. He moved back to Linton five years ago with his wife Margaret to whom he has been married for sixty one years. The couple have six children, ten grandchildren and two great grandchildren and now live at the Fountaine Hospital.

Parking near to Linton church is provided at a charge but, as there is so much to see in the vicinity, it's well worth it, especially as you can also cross the footbridge and walk the short distance to Grassington. Once you've enjoyed a view of Linton falls, call in at the beautiful St Michael and All Angels church, whose history goes back before the time of the Norman Conquest, though what survives today ranges

Pensioner Robert Chaney
has seen many a mist
come in over Wharfedale

from the twelfth century onwards. The fact that the church is so squat, as protection against inclement weather, is actually part of its appeal: it feels rooted in its Yorkshire earth and stone. Downstream from the church are stepping stones, regularly used on drier days: and in the field opposite the church is an unusual standing stone, if you have time to go and investigate.

Our day had sadly come to a close long before we could explore the further treasures of one of Yorkshire's most famous and rewarding of river valleys. However, Wharfedale and its many wonders repay its visitors along the full sixty miles of the river from its source on Cam Fell in Langstrothdale to its conjunction with the Ouse near to Cawood. Several days, if not a whole lifetime, barely do it justice: small wonder that Robert Chaney has chosen to spend more than eighty years living here.

Fact File

The Fox and Hounds
Starbotton, North Yorkshire
BD23 5HY
☎ 01756 760269
🖰www.foxandhounds-starbotton.com
*Open Tuesday to Sunday. B &B
accommodation available.*

The Blue Bell Inn
Kettlewell, North Yorkshire
BD23 5QX
☎ 01756 760230
🖰www.bluebellkettlewell.co.uk
B&B accommodation available.

Zarina's Tea Room
Middle Lane, Kettlewell,
North Yorkshire BD23 5QX
☎ 01756 761188
🖰www.kettlewell.info
B&B accommodation available.

Buckden Village website
🖰www.buckden.org

The Fountaine Inn
Linton, North Yorkshire BD23 5HJ
☎ 01756 752210
🖰www.fountaineinnatlinton.co.uk
Accommodation available.

161

The River Ure
where it joins
the River Cover

THE FORGOTTEN DALE
Coverdale (June)

The gateway to Coverdale, one of the loveliest yet least known of Yorkshire's delightful dales, is Kettlewell, which nestles at the foot of Park Rash, the first part of the narrow road that snakes its way up hill and down dale following the River Cover on its journey to join the Ure in Wensleydale. Kettlewell, one of Upper Wharfedale's finest villages, and famed for its starring role in the film *Calendar Girls*, perhaps needs little extra attention, but the tiny hamlets and villages of calendar-picture Coverdale have retained a strange anonymity for far too long.

It has been said of Coverdale that it takes a Yorkshireman to find it, but even he doesn't know where it is. Most people passing through Kettlewell northwards are on their way to Buckden, or Aysgarth, or Hawes. But by taking the time to explore Kettlewell a little further, there is no real difficulty in finding the much less travelled road to Middleham and Leyburn – and you won't regret making that choice.

Amazingly, this narrow road (too small to be given a designated number) was, in past centuries, a major highway, part of the main stagecoach route between the capital of the north, Richmond, and London. There can have been no more dangerous a stretch of road for man and horse alike in the entire two hundred and fifty mile journey given the precipitous downslope from Tor Pike Pass (the road's highest point) as one approaches Kettlewell along Park Rash from the north. Even a modern motor vehicle struggles to climb the twisting and turning lane heading towards Middleham – but the effort is definitely worth it.

Within minutes of our leaving Kettlewell behind, we felt as if we were off the beaten track entering what seemed like an entirely uninhabited landscape. The moorland mountain of Great Whernside dominates the view to the east, with regular rivulets, like herring bones, feeding into the spine of the River Cover. To the west lies the imposing North Moor, with its gurgling gills cascading in winter, trickling in summer – and too treacherous a terrain for walkers. This is hardy farmers' land, the only buildings for some miles being field barns and occasional millstone grit farmhouses.

The first settlement you pass through is Braidley, with its own Moor to the left, Arkleside Moor to the right. It is little more than a collection of rugged farm dwellings, testament to the robustness of its residents. But before too long you reach the comforts of Horsehouse, its name betraying its origins as a staging post.

Its inn, the charmingly old-fashioned Thwaite Arms, post office and its church, St Botolph's, offer sanctuary from the previous five miles of apparent isolation – and such is its beauty that it has succumbed to the potential peril of the affluent second-home owner. Its appeal to the weekender is all too obvious – who wouldn't want this beautiful landscape regularly in view? – but it would be a shame if such settlements became ghost villages for most of the week.

We met one of the villagers, a friendly chap whose accent betrayed his Essex origins. He told us that he had been evacuated to Yorkshire during the war and had fallen in love with the landscape. 'It's lovely that I've ended up back here. There really is no better place to be; especially on a day like today.' He was right – the warm sun of a bright June day added gloriously to the Dale's natural beauty.

As you approach Carlton, the countryside noticeably softens in nature. It's worth diverting from the main route briefly to visit the hamlet of West Scrafton, noted for its tiny triangular chain-posted village green, and to understand why James Herriot regularly holidayed here. It was quite clear he was no mere weekender – the

The road through Coverdale

chapter on Coverdale in his book *James Herriot's Yorkshire* demonstrates his deep-rooted attachment to this most enchanting of hideaways.

You could venture further along this road, to Caldbergh and to Coverham, with views west to Penhill, and the Roova Crag on the eastern skyline, or you could double back to appreciate the appeal of the daleside's largest habitation, Carlton, boasting a sizeable inn (the Foresters Arms), a house with a mounted cartwheel, and a poetry-emblazoned front wall. Flatts Farm must be one of very few houses in the country bearing a poetic plaque, in this case dedicated to Henry Constantine, 'the Coverdale bard', and dated February 1861.

This really is walking country with routes over Melmerby Moor towards West Burton in Bishopdale, or south-east towards Nidderdale, or east towards Masham, so don't forget to have your hiking boots in the back of the car. Once you've passed through Carlton, and a little before you might choose to branch off to Coverham, you will encounter signs for The Forbidden Corner at Tupgill Park. What is forbidden is simply to turn up. You have to book in advance by phoning or you can buy tickets from the tourist information offices at Leyburn and Middleham.

The Forbidden Corner bills itself as 'a unique labyrinth of tunnels, chambers, follies and surprises created in a four acre garden in the heart of the Yorkshire Dales' and has recently won an award as the best children's attraction in Yorkshire. Youngsters are likely to be enthralled by its mixture of underworld temple, translucent glass pyramid, paths and passages that lead nowhere and extraordinary statues – it's a sizeable maze of riddle-solving and exploration.

As we wanted to save delightful, historic Middleham until last, we followed the eastbound single track road beyond Coverham and its ruined abbey. You'll notice the impressive seventeenth century Braithwaite Hall on the hill to your right, and be yet more impressed to discover it offers bed and breakfast.

Continuing east you arrive, unsurprisingly, at East Witton with its enchanting long rows of mainly nineteenth century cottages either side of a wide green. One of East Witton's treasures is its inn, The Blue Lion, widely considered to be one of the best dining establishments in Yorkshire. We decided it was our duty to check out its credentials, so we refreshed ourselves with chilled white wine, and chose from the list of starters for a light lunch – grilled goat's cheese on hazelnut toast with roasted red peppers, and king scallops in a lemon and spring onion risotto. It was all delicious; a stop here is thoroughly recommended.

By following the A6108 due north for half a mile, you reach the Cover Bridge Inn where we turned off briefly across the bridge to Ulshaw. From the bridge you have a view of the conjoining of the Ure and the Cover but another reason for stopping is to explore the grounds of St Simon and St Jude. This architecturally quirky Catholic church is almost hidden behind a tall eighteenth century dwelling, but its turret-like spire will instantly intrigue you. Entrance to the churchyard is gained through a grave-lined pathway towards an imposing life-size figure of Christ on the cross.

We returned to the main road and drove west, taking the turn left into the town of Middleham, built on rising land between the Ure and the Cover. Middleham is famed for its race horses and gallops, for its twelfth century castle, once the home of Richard the Third, and for its generous supply of inns surrounding the market square, including a pub now called The Richard the Third – and there's a Black Bull, and both a Black Swan and a White Swan. Coach travellers were in no danger of inadequate watering here. The view of the castle from the south just before entering the town is particularly impressive. The partially ruined castle is now maintained by English Heritage, so don't forget your membership cards, if you have them. Entrance is reasonably priced if you're not a member – and it was one of James Herriot's favourite spots.

You can return to Kettlewell by retracing the route through Coverdale, or by joining the A684 west and branching off south-west into Bishopdale via Cray, Buckden and Starbotton on the B6160. Alternatively, you could drive south-east from Middleham on the A684 which would bring you to Masham and eventually to the A1.

Of course, a day here is not enough and you will want to keep coming back. Coverdale may be the so-called 'forgotten dale', but once you've found it you'll never, ever forget it.

Fact File

The Blue Lion Inn
East Witton, Nr Leyburn,
North Yorkshire DL8 4SN
☎ 01969 624273
🖰www.thebluelion.co.uk

Braithwaite Hall
East Witton, North Yorkshire
DL8 4SY
☎ 01969 640287
🖰www.yorkshirenet.co.uk

The Thwaite Arms
Horsehouse,
North Yorkshire DL8 4TS
☎ 01969 640206

The Foresters Arms
Carlton-in-Coverdale,
North Yorkshire DL8 4BB
☎ 01969 640272
🖰www.forestersarms-carlton.co.uk

Bus information
☎ 0870 6082 608
🖰www.dalesbus.org

The Forbidden Corner
Tupgill Park Estate,
Coverham, North Yorkshire
DL8 4TJ
☎ 01969 640638
🖰www.theforbiddencorner.co.uk

The view
towards
Littondale

THE 'BRIGHT STREAM' DALE
Littondale (July)

'A quiet, silent, rich, happy place; a narrow crack cut deep into the earth; so deep, and so out of the way...' Thus begins the second chapter of Charles Kingsley's *The Water Babies*.

It continues: 'The name of the place is Vendale; and if you want to see it for yourself, you must go up into the High Craven... north by Ingleborough, to the Nine Standards and Cross Fell; and if you have not found it, you must turn south, and search the Lake Mountains, down to Scaw Fell and the sea; and then, if you have not found it, you must go northward again by merry Carlisle, and search the Cheviots all across... and then, whether you have found Vendale or not, you will have found such a country, and such a people, as ought to make you proud of being a British boy.'

What Kingsley termed Vendale is in fact our Littondale, and is a great deal easier to find than he suggests – just turn left after Kilnsey Crag as you head north. Kilnsey Crag, just north of Grassington, is renowned among climbers for its forty foot overhang, and for its ever circling and swooping summer swifts. This limestone promontory juts out its snout towards the roadside like a gigantic sea mammal, making it an unmistakeable landmark.

Occasional motorists might take the fork left just before the Skirfare

Bridge, assuming it to be the continuation of the Upper Wharfedale road to Kettlewell. They would be wrong, but their delight at discovering the tucked away village of Arncliffe some five miles further on would more than make up for the mistake.

To reach this rural retreat, the narrow road winds between craggy flanks, hemmed in further by well-kept dry-stone walls. Sheep and cows graze in the pastures, often in the same field. The hills either side are not towering crags, dominating the horizon, but are somehow more proportionate, less dramatic perhaps, but also easier on the eye than elsewhere in the deeper dales.

Littondale is one of the few Yorkshire dales to be named after a village rather than its river. 'Skirfaredale' doesn't exactly trip off the tongue, though the beauty of this delightful dale might leave you temporarily tongue-tied. Its river (whose name derives from the Scandanavian for 'bright stream') can sometimes be a raging torrent though, when we visited, it was, in places, little more than a trickle. A fictional version of the Skirfare is where Kingsley's Tom, the chimney sweep, first entered the water to begin his adventure.

Kilnsey
Crag

The Queen's
Arms at Litton

Above the village of Litton, in the higher reaches of the Skirfare, the river seems to disappear altogether, leaving a rocky bed. When water levels are low, the river at this point follows an underground course.

At Arncliffe, the river conjoins with Cowside Beck which has its source high up on Fountains Fell. Arncliffe (its name means 'where eagles perch on the cliff') almost, but not quite, appropriately boasts a pub called The Falcon, which was the location for The Woolpack in the earliest outdoor shots for the long-running TV series *Emmerdale*. It is likely the soap opera derived its name from Wordsworth's name for the dale – Amerdale – as used in his famous long poem *The White Doe of Rylstone*. Arncliffe's community building is called Amerdale Hall and the renowned hotel (once famed for its food but now, sadly, closed) was called Amerdale House Hotel. The spot where the Skirfare and the Wharfe conjoin is also known locally as Amerdale Dub.

You find the time-frozen inn, The Falcon, at the top end of Arncliffe's impressive village green. The hugely appealing interior of the pub looks like it hasn't been altered since at least before the Second World War. There are royal coats of arms, bench seating, corner

Arncliffe
stocks

cupboards and what looks like an ancient walnut pew. A glimpse into the kitchen reveals an Aga and Victorian-style ceiling drying rack. The cosy and inviting residents' lounge could easily be used as a period film set. An age-old tradition here, which always causes comment, is that beer is still served direct from the keg into an earthenware jug before being poured into your glass. Robin Miller and his wife have been running the pub since 1976 and, in fact, he grew up there, his father having run the pub before him.

Robin regrets that they no longer film *Emmerdale* at Arncliffe having enjoyed the company of 'the film folk'. As for Arncliffe's future, he's pleased that it has a life beyond catering for holiday-makers and that there's a genuine sense of community. 'A village is only as good as the folk that live there,' comments Robin, the inference being that Arncliffe is, indeed, a very good place to live.

As you head up the dale out of the village, the Skirfare passes under a beautiful arched road bridge close to St Oswald's Church, with its Celtic cross gravestones. The present church dates from 1841 but is built on Norman foundations and has a fifteenth century tower. Inside, a soldier's pike is displayed and a list of local men who fought at Flodden Field in 1513. Local legend has it that they garnered the yew for their bows from Yew Cogar Scar, Cowside Beck's ravine. Just outside the churchyard are some stocks, now restored, which suggest that, even in a paradise such as Arncliffe, there must once have been sinners.

Litton, the next village as you head north-west, disconcertingly has a name which means 'the village on a torrent', which was certainly not the case on this particular day. Drinkers and diners lounged in the sunshine at tables outside The Queen's Arms. It must be even more inviting in winter, however, when a roaring fire in the oak-beamed bar would provide a cheery welcome to weary walkers.

The pub is a lovely building which helps sustain the few other village houses, some of which look like holiday homes. The friendly barman told us about the pub's history. 'There has been a building here since the sixteen hundreds but it has only been a pub since 1841.' Standing in the cosy front bar, it is possible to see which parts are original and which parts have been added on. The outside walls are more than three feet thick in places and the two period windows at the front are not quite level. The Queen's Arms has a microbrewery in the back where they brew their own beer as well as supplying five other pubs. Four different ales are produced, though Litton Ale is their mainstay and is thoroughly recommended.

Continuing north-west you arrive at Halton Gill, where the former school is now rented out – on the day we were there a party was taking place with a bouncy castle for the children – and the church (still with its bell-tower) is now a private residence. At the head of the dale is Foxup, where Foxup Beck and Cosh Beck meet to become the Skirfare. Here you will find four stone bridges which allow access from the road to dwellings and barns. And once you've found Foxup, there remains only one thing to do – put on your walking boots and hike over Foxup Moor and Plover Hill to Pen-y-ghent, one of the three famous Yorkshire peaks.

There are innumerable walks that start in Littondale. Perhaps the most famous and most demanding, incorporating both Arncliffe and Litton, is The Walk around the Ulfkil Stride, formerly a thirty-three mile challenge walk (now reduced to twenty-five miles) over the fells

Kilnsey Crag features in many a stunning Wharfedale view

of Upper Wharfedale created in 1979 by the late Jack Rayner, a member of the West Yorkshire Group of the Long Distance Walkers Association who now run this event once a year.

On the day of our all too brief visit, we retraced our route by driving back to Arncliffe and taking the left fork. Keeping the river on your right, you are immediately rewarded with some of the best roadside views in the dale as you head towards the lovely hamlet of Hawkswick; there's no better place for gentle walks by the river in the dappling shade of the trees. As you head back towards Wharfedale, the view opens out upon an ideal picnic spot with a vista towards Kilnsey Crag that is a must for all landscape photographers.

So, demonstrating the innate generosity of Yorkshire folk, you get three dales here for the price of one: Amerdale, Vendale and, of course, Littondale.

Fact File

The Falcon Inn
Arncliffe, North Yorkshire
BD23 5QE
☎ 01756 770205

The Queens Arms
Litton, North Yorkshire BD23 5QJ
☎ 01756 770208
🖱www.yorkshirenet.co.uk

Stonelands Farmyard
holiday cottages (*just outside Litton*)
☎ 01756 770293 or visit
🖱www.stonelands.co.uk

Halton Gill Bunk Barn
☎ 01756 770241

SWALEDALE
AND NEIGHBOURS

Birk Dale, Whitsundale, Upper Swaledale, West Stonesdale, Arkengarthdale

A derelict barn
and pens in
Birk Dale

THE GLORIOUS DALE
Birk Dale (October)

Birk Dale (sometimes spelt as one word) isn't the most northerly of the dales we have so much enjoyed visiting, though it sometimes feels like it. During two out of three recent trips here the weather was cloudy, cold and uninviting even in late summer and early autumn. However, when the sun shines there can be few places quite so glorious, quite so visually stunning.

Our means of approaching this remote outpost of the Yorkshire Dales National Park was via Hawes, in Wensleydale, then following the giddy and unnerving C road up (and up and onwards) over the famous Buttertubs Pass, descending to Swaledale, with Muker in view eastwards and with Thwaite to the left.

Taking this left turn (you are now on the B6270, Swaledale's main thoroughfare, leading you to Reeth and towards Richmond in one direction, and to Natesby and towards Kirkby Stephen in the other) you immediately find yourself in the small, quietly charming yet imposing village of Thwaite.

Several of the houses in Thwaite advertise themselves as holiday cottages and the village is indeed a lovely place to use as a base for exploring an area of outstanding beauty. We got chatting to a man who was sanding down his front door who described himself as 'an incomer' and has owned a holiday property in the village for twenty years. We asked him if he knew anything about the famous flash flood in Thwaite at the end of the nineteenth century. He joked that he hadn't actually been around at the time but had heard the bridge had been washed away by the torrents. Fortunately no-one had been killed but the event lived on in folklore. He advised us to talk to a local man known as Jack Ned. 'He was born in that house,' he said pointing to a small stone cottage. 'And now he lives in that one,' he added, indicating another cottage just round the corner.

Jack, in his mid-eighties, has lived in Thwaite all his life. 'I've never lived anywhere else and I've no desire to.' He has travelled to Scotland and Wales but not 'over the water'. He has farmed at Thwaite and Keld and worked for landowners Lord Peel and Lord Arundel as a gamekeeper on their estates. He has also, in his time, been a butcher, a stonemason and an undertaker's assistant. Jack Ned (full name John Edward Reynoldson) confirmed the earlier account of the flood but with this further vital detail: 'A pig got took but it got out further down river.'

The Kearton Country Hotel, Tea Room, Gift Shop and Beer Garden in Thwaite is a very warm and friendly place to stop off – the sign at the front encouragingly announces: 'Muddy boots welcome', good to know if you have been walking the Pennine Way which runs through the village. The view out onto the moor – the purple of the heather quite startling even in the dampness and mist – was all the more appealing for the tessellated patterns created by the dry stone walls.

The hotel is named after Thwaite-born brothers Richard and Cherry Kearton who, between them, were famous for wildlife writing and daring photography at the end of the nineteenth century and in the first part of the twentieth century. Their pioneering endeavours, especially in the sphere of early film-making in spectacular settings, are the perfect example of how a fascination with the wild can lift the human spirit.

Heading north out of the village the next settlement is Angram, distinguished by a celtic-style stone with the name of the hamlet vertically engraved upon it. It boasts the date AD 807 but the carving and construction of the stone would appear to be of much later origin. Already, Swaledale is narrowing at this point to what feels more like an

Birkdale
tarn

enclosing gorge than a dale. However, the landscape opens up to some extent as you approach Keld, a village located off the main road but linked by two lanes to the east and west which form a neat triangle. There's bed and breakfast facilities here (for example, at Butt House), as well as a caravan and camping enterprise whose customers are privileged to enjoy breathtaking scenery on their temporary doorsteps.

Keld Lodge, formerly a Youth Hostel, is now a thriving hotel and hostelry run by Linda Birkett and her partner Tony Leete. They bought it in October 2006, carried out extensive renovation work and opened the following Easter. It has been a successful business ever since. The lodge is on the Coast to Coast walk, the Pennine Way and the Land's End to John O'Groats walk, among others.

'We are on the route of about ten walks, so it's mostly walkers we have staying,' says Linda. 'But we get lots of local people coming to the restaurant. The last time there was a pub in Keld was in 1954 – so the locals are very happy.' There were plans to start up a microbrewery to be called Kelda breweries. 'You have to love people in this business,' says Linda. 'And we do.'

A Day In A Dale

It was Linda who told us about Ravenseat Farm where the farmer's wife, Amanda, sells teas and homemade scones. 'She's a shepherdess. She's amazing – she has three children and she wants six. She makes the scones and serves the teas with a baby on her back. All she wants to do is look after her sheep and have children. She's tall and blonde – really beautiful: her mother was a model.' We made a note to ourselves to make a visit – it was the word 'scones' that did it.

Continuing past Park Bridge, prepare to gasp and then gasp some more. This stretch of the upper reaches of the River Swale, close to the roadside, provides splendid views of Wain Wath Falls and other lesser waterfalls, with an escarpment backdrop that is a must for the happy snapper and professional photographer alike.

The next obvious turning to the right is signposted to the Tolkienesque place name of Ravenseat, one and a quarter miles to the north. If you stay on the main road – which by now feels to be little more than a track – you are about to encounter Birk Dale proper, but it would be a fool indeed who did not make the excursion to Ravenseat Farm where you will meet Amanda. To access the picnic area you have to cross a ford in a car or over a stone bridge on foot. In good weather, it's an absolutely idyllic setting. We got out of the car and went to the

'Do you want some?' Tups at Ravenseat

farmhouse where there was a bell at the door to ring for service. We rang the bell and waited; when there was no reply, we headed back to the car. Children in the distance started waving to us and broke into a run, so we stopped the car for a quick chat. They were extremely friendly, and one of them ran off 'to get the adults.' Amanda arrived bearing a handsome baby boy in a carry-pack on her back and holding a steel rod contraption in her hand which turned out to be a mole catching device. 'We've been on a mole hunt,' she grinned, gleefully showing us a dead mole in one of her pockets. She, her husband Clive Owen, and three children were all extremely welcoming. As we talked we learned that they farm over a thousand sheep and a small number of cattle, while the tea and scones business is a sociable sideline.

'I don't fit the archetypal image of a farmer's wife,' laughed Amanda. 'I'm a shepherdess and I only came here ten years ago to borrow a tup, a ram, off Clive. I stayed. I started to do the teas and scones this year and it's been really interesting – we have met all kinds of people. One guy who came for a cup of tea said that, with the hills and all the children running around, it was like the *Sound of Music* here.'

Retracing your route, however reluctantly, back to the main thoroughfare, the road to Natesby is by now heading more westerly

The sunshine
breaks through at
Wain Wath Falls

Lifelong
Thwaite
resident
Jack Ned

than north. At this stage of the journey, you very definitely feel that you are in some of the most isolated outreaches of the Dales.

At about this point bird watchers might well want to park their cars and put on their walking boots. With the use of a good map you can locate Birkdale Tarn, which is not much more than two hundred metres from the road but there are no marked footpaths and there is a bit of a climb to negotiate. The tarn is the third largest in Yorkshire – it's about three hundred and fifty metres across at its widest point and is the perfect place, on a clear day, for spotting moorland birds.

Just south of the tarn is the confluence of Great Sleddale Beck and Birkdale Beck, marking the source of the River Swale on its journey eastwards. The next few miles westwards take you into the heart of glorious Birk Dale with barely an inhabited dwelling in sight. There are 'field' barns (without the fields) scattered about the moorland wilderness. Close to the road you'll come upon a moss-covered example of just such a barn, though this one is remarkable for having a chimney and a network of stone-wall pens to the front and side. To left and right, assuming the mists have not come down, as they are apt to, there are great expanses of moorland grasses and heather.

The road west and north leads you out of North Yorkshire and into Cumbria and it is recommended that you continue a little way to let your eyes drink in the sudden view – as you round a bend at the top of Tailbrig Hill – over the Eden Valley. The relative flatness of the plain in contrast to the terrain which has surrounded you throughout the length of Upper Swaledale and Birk Dale is perhaps part of the surprise. Without doubt, the sky seems 'big' here – the combination of being quite so high above the valley, along with the great distances that open up before you, is truly a pleasure to the eye as well as to one's enduring memories.

Fact File

Kearton Country Hotel
Thwaite, North Yorkshire
DL11 6DR
☎ 01748 886277
www.keartoncountryhotel.co.uk

Butt House (*bed and breakfast*)
Keld, North Yorkshire
☎ 01748 886374
www.coasttocoastguides.co.uk

Keld Lodge
Keld, North Yorkshire DL11 6LL
☎ 01748 886259
www.keldlodge.com

Park Lodge campsite
Keld, North Yorkshire DL11 6LJ
☎ 01748 886274
www.rukins-keld.co.uk

Park House campsite and Keld Bunkhouse
Park House, Keld,
North Yorkshire DL11 6DZ
☎ 01748 886549
www.keldbunkhouse.com

Ravenseat Farm
☎ 01748 886387
www.ravenseat.com

Best explored
on foot -
Whitsundale

THE WILDERNESS DALE
Whitsundale (June)

Named after a religious festival – Whitsun being the seventh Sunday after Easter Sunday – this picturesque dale can only be explored on foot, and what better time to set out on such an adventure than during the Whitsun holiday? Whitsun is traditionally a time for walks and processions, especially in the North East – perhaps that is how the dale originally got its name – and so it seemed appropriate that we should pull on our hiking boots on the Friday before Whit Sunday to spend a day walking the length of Whitsundale. For once we were blessed with wonderful weather; the sun shone down on us for the whole day and we met other Whit walkers along the way, many of them following the immortal Wainwright's Coast to Coast long-distance walk.

Whitsundale (pronounced 'Wizzendul' locally) is arguably Yorkshire's most remote dale. It's located in a tucked-away sheep-grazing hideaway not far from Upper Swaledale and Birk Dale. There is no road access within the dale, and its northern approach can only be arrived at after a trek along the Coast to Coast route from Kirkby Stephen. Its southern tip, however, accommodates Ravenseat Farm, accessible by a single track road, and famous to walkers for Amanda's cream teas. Amanda Owen, who we first met on one of our Day in a Dale trips to Birk Dale, has now appeared on TV, radio and in a variety

A Day In A Dale

Ravenseat bridge

of newspaper and magazine articles. Amanda is one of the region's true characters ('Fame hasn't changed me,' she deadpans) and it was good to catch up with her again. The first time we met her, she had three children, with ambitions for three more: she now has five, so can the sixth be far behind?

As we drove through Upper Swaledale, northwards, a car passed us with the unmistakeable Amanda at the wheel. We were a little surprised, having expected to meet her at Ravenseat within a matter of minutes. It wasn't the only surprise on our journey: a hare loping down the road, a day-time owl hunting above Sleddale and clouds of temperature-inversion induced mists over Gayle and Hawes added interest to the already glorious views on our journey. When we arrived at the farm, we were greeted by Clive, Amanda's husband, and the children, with the news that Amanda was taking her fourth child, then a ten-month old infant, to the doctor's at Hawes because of a chest infection. Though concerned, we were also keen to begin our walk in the wilderness dale that is Whitsundale and Clive very kindly offered to drive us towards Kirkby Stephen so that we could make a start.

Clive admits that he is not a map reader but we were not too anxious when he went past a signposted route towards the Nine Standards and dropped us off further north at a spot which afforded stunning views over Cumbria and the Eden Valley. However, after ten minutes of walking we realised that there was no sign of a designated path to the cairns we had chosen to be our 'starting' point, which meant scrambling over walls and becks and up steep slopes before we worked out more precisely where we were on the map. It was also helpful that we bumped into a couple of walkers from Canada who were by-passing the Nine Standards en route to Keld and whose directions were able to confirm that we were not quite as lost as we feared. Even so, by the time we arrived at the top of the ridge we were around an hour behind our estimated schedule.

The Nine Standards, beautifully crafted cairns which have withstood centuries of tempests and torrents, have given their name to the hill on which they stand some six hundred and sixty metres above sea level. Nine Standards Rigg is a literal watershed of a hill for, east of this ridge, waters flow towards the North Sea, while westwards they flow towards the Irish Sea. On the day of our visit, much of the water had decided to stay precisely where it was, adding to the notoriously boggy conditions on the paths.

The Standards themselves appear to be the result of a zany contest to see who could build a ten foot cairn in a geometrical design distinct from any other. They stand on the former boundary between Yorkshire and Cumberland – which may well explain why they were built in the first place. However, myths abound as to their original purpose – they are certainly more than two hundred years old, as verified by historical maps – and many support the idea that they were built to suggest a camp of soldiers, serving to ward off invaders from the North. They are also the perfect spot for a picnic.

After a brief bite to eat, we had a chat with an American couple, Bert and Jean Hammons, who had travelled all the way from Wisconsin to walk the Coast to Coast route. They have done several long-distance walks in Europe, three of them in Britain. 'We really enjoy being out in the countryside,' said Jean. 'It's delightful to see people, particularly young people, out walking because it just doesn't happen in the States.' They were also impressed by the hospitality of the people running the bed and breakfasts they were staying in. 'It's great to be able to walk from one overnight stay to another,' said Bert. 'We don't have that kind of structure at home because the distances in between are just too large.'

We followed the 'blue' route past the trig marker and made our unseasonal journey towards Whitsundale, unseasonal because you are advised to follow particular paths (designated red, blue and green) at certain times of the year, and the Whitsundale route is for August to November. We, of course, wanted to see the dale during the Whitsun week itself and had chosen the very best of weather for our explorations. However, preceding weeks had been rather wet and, whichever route we had taken, the bogginess of the path, particularly when crossing the numerous rills that bisect the terrain, would have made progress quite tricky. Good walking boots are essential – and probably a change of clothing. We were also very grateful for the regular marker posts without which we could have strayed into potential difficulties: this, but for the path, is pretty wild country.

With views from above Birkdale Tarn in the distance, we gradually descended into the northern tip of the dale where the beck meanders in

The Nine Standards on the Coast to Coast Walk

The beck meanders through Whitsundale

textbook fashion and the valley is at its flattest and widest. A bluff above the meander, with bird's eye views of the water's course, is a perfect resting point or lunch spot. The beckside is punctuated by occasional sheepfolds though, prior to arriving at the stream, we had not seen a single living thing apart from the lapwings screeching overhead, protective of their ground nests. At one point we startled a grouse, though it was probably less startled than we were. The Coast to Coast route here follows the beck on its west bank, with no sign of human habitation for miles. This is the valley that Wainwright referred to as 'desolation profound.'

You are now into gentle walking country, secure in the knowledge that just by following the beck you are guaranteed to arrive at Ravenseat without losing your way. The beck itself continues to wind and bend, its clear brown waters suggestive of pale ale. In time, it is possible to make out field barns on the horizon, the first indication that the farm is not far away.

After the beautiful bleakness of Whitsundale, Ravenseat is a welcome oasis, surrounded by a sea of yellow marsh marigolds and low hills. Clive, concerned that we might have got lost, had been quizzing the various walkers who had arrived for tea and scones. But for being reassured that we had been spotted en route, he would have come in search of us: however, we'd made good time along the dale itself and caught up with those who had followed the 'red' route more appropriate for the time of year.

As we climbed our last wall, Amanda roared into view on her quad bike, racing off to a field barn to collect eggs. Amanda combines her role as a shepherdess, mother, baker, waitress and media celebrity with aplomb and her next venture is to provide overnight accommodation for Coast to Coast walkers. She was also happy to advertise her willingness to make arrangements for potential Whitsundale walkers to park their car at Ravenseat and be driven by her to the signposted route to the Nine Standards for a small contribution to expenses. That way, as long as you have food, fitness and footwear, you can follow in our footsteps just as we have followed in Wainwright's.

Fact File
A Day in a Dale

Coast to Coast Walk
www.coast2coast.co.uk

Ravenseat Farm
Cream teas with homemade scones available as well as cold drinks. There is also a Shepherd's Hut available for overnight accommodation.
☎ 01748 886387.
www.ravenseat.com

Walking routes
The 'green' route (December to April) avoids the Nine Standards altogether; the 'red' route is May to July, and the 'blue' route – which includes Whitsundale – is August to November.

Keld Lodge
Keld, North Yorkshire, DL11 6LL
☎ 01748 886259
www.keldlodge.com

The valley
of the barns
- Swaledale

THE WILDFLOWERS AND WALKERS DALE
Upper Swaledale (October)

Having been to Swaledale for the Muker Show at the beginning of September in glorious sunshine, it was only fair, perhaps, that our day in the dale later in the year should prove to be a wet and dismal day of weather: it's a kind of equilibrium. Even so, Swaledale has plenty to offer; in fact, one day is hardly enough to do justice to all there is to see.

We travelled out of Wensleydale via Askrigg, avoiding the Buttertubs Pass which had been closed for repairs. Near High Oxnop we met four hardy and sensibly dressed students taking part in an expedition as part of the Duke of Edinburgh Gold award scheme. Sixth formers at the Grammar School at Leeds, they were on day three of a four day trek and were heading for Hardraw having left their campsite at Keld at seven-thirty that morning. 'The weather's been a bit miserable,' said one of them, but added, indicating the view, 'It's pretty stunning looking back the way we've come.'

Lower down the hill, at Crow Trees, the road is remarkably steep as it descends to the main road through Swaledale, the B6270, and you thank your lucky stars and regular servicing that the brakes on the car are reliable. We turned left, drove through Muker and on to the other end of the Buttertubs road to discover that it had in fact re-opened –

and this was to be the beginning of our own expedition through Swaledale, on four wheels. No Gold award for our means of travel.

Swaledale actually begins further up the dale, beyond Keld, but our first stopping point was at the waterfalls close to the road at Scar Houses. The beck here is not the River Swale, which doesn't enter this part of the valley until east of Muker. The falls belong to Straw Beck and were particularly appealing following heavy overnight rain. In the adjoining field a Swaledale sheep posed quite brazenly at the top of the brow, not moving until his photo had been snapped.

We parked in the car park at the eastern end of Muker to enjoy a stroll around the village. Look out for the sheep on a roof (though more of that kind of thing anon), the giant chair outside the crafts shop and the clever shadow effect of the pub name, The Farmers Arms – if the sun is shining. As elsewhere in the dale, Muker has a Literary Institute which predates the provision of lending libraries. Muker had become a prosperous village in the late nineteenth century thanks to the lead mining industry; and the Literary Institute, with its incongruously ornate style, was built in 1867 from public subscription. By the end of the century it contained six hundred books. The village church, St Mary's, is a beautifully simple and peaceful place of worship, known as a chapel of ease, erected in 1580 with substantial rebuilding in the eighteenth and nineteenth centuries. Before the construction of St Mary's, the only church in the dale was St Andrew's at Grinton which meant that coffins had to be carried as far as fifteen miles along what was known as the Corpse Way.

Just north of Muker is Ivelet Side, which fell runners tackle with giddying athleticism during the Muker Show. The hamlet of Ivelet lies further to the east, perched above the Swale and reached by a lane off the main road leading to a narrow, elegant centuries-old bridge. There's no signpost, so you need a map or local knowledge to find the bridge which, in better weather, would make an ideal picnic spot. What might put you off your sandwich, however, is the legend that the bridge is haunted by a headless hound which leaps over the parapet into the Swale as a spookily spectacular means of predicting a dreadful fate for anyone who sees this paranormal phenomenon. We didn't.

In Gunnerside, we felt the need of some late morning refreshment, not having picnicked in the rain at the bridge, so we called in at the

The River Swale and Whitsundale beck converge

Ghyllfoot Tearoom where Linda Le Cuirot and her husband Bob, who is from Jersey, have been providing hot drinks, snacks and meals for twenty-five years. 'I was born and brought up in Gunnerside,' says Linda. Her maiden name is Calvert – one of the well-known Dales names – and her father was the local blacksmith. 'I love it here; I wouldn't want to move away,' she says. 'My parents still live here and my siblings are close by.' Remarkably, Linda has the knack of remembering customers from one year to the next, however infrequently they might visit, and she can even recall what they ordered. 'Quite often they'll have exactly what they had before!' she laughs.

In the tea-room we also met husband and wife Pete and Chris, originally from Hull, who now live in Healaugh. 'We love the Dales,' says Pete. 'We had been coming up here for years – we had a holiday cottage in Langthwaite – and then about ten years ago we decided to relocate up here.' Both now retired, Chris says that they are enjoying exploring the Dales. 'Swaledale is special, though,' she says. 'When we have been out for the day, it's always lovely to come back to Swaledale – it's homely and peaceful and a little bit wild.' On the day we met them, they had caught the bus to Thwaite and were walking back through the dale, following the river, and had stopped off at Linda's for some refreshment and shelter from the drizzle outside, though there was plenty of lemon drizzle inside.

Gunnerside sits high above the Swale after a huge bend in the road, and has its own beck running through the village at right angles to the river until they conjoin, swelling the Swale, at Gunnerside New Bridge. Driving eastwards into Low Row, we took the opportunity to visit the

One of Straw Beck's many waterfalls in Swaledale

newly spruced-up Punch Bowl Inn, which was proving popular with the lunchtime trade. The transformation is remarkable: now it retains the best of the old, feels light and airy, and offers gastropub fare and good quality bed and breakfast accommodation. If some of its décor reminds you of the CB Inn in Arkengarthdale, that is no real surprise as it is run by the same owners, Charles and Stacy Cody.

Healaugh is a hamlet without shops, tea-rooms or pubs, but worthy of note is its telephone box. Someone has taken the trouble to furnish it with a small square of carpet and a vase of fresh wildflowers. Another feature of the old red GPO box is that it is used as the collection point for newspapers delivered to the village.

We have visited Reeth many times, because of the museum, the annual pantomime and its being the gateway into Arkengarthdale. Helen Bainbridge, who runs the Swaledale Museum, recommended we try the White House tearooms if ever we were visiting the village, so we popped in for a bite to eat and a cup of tea. Richard and John, who run the tea-rooms just off the village green, have decorated the interior with wallpaper that might convince the short-sighted they are

The River Swale near Kisdon Hill

in the library of a Victorian cottage. Floral displays and fine china crockery announce that you have arrived in a refined establishment where light snacks and more substantial meals are served with close regard to quality, presentation and wholesomeness.

We chatted to Joyce and Arthur from Darlington who are regular customers. They love Swaledale, having had a holiday cottage in Low Row for forty years and the White House has become a favourite venue for family celebrations – indeed, they were booking up for Joyce's birthday next March.

Beyond Fremington, and over yet another Swale bridge, this time at the Bridge Inn at Grinton, you can explore inside and around the grounds of one of the finest medieval churches anywhere in the country. St Andrew's at Grinton is known as 'the Cathedral of the Dales' and it's easy to understand why – apart from its size. It's a magnificent church with high vaulted ceilings and spectacular stained glass windows. It was originally built around 1100 by the monks of Bridlington and provided a place of worship for surrounding villages in the dale.

In Grinton we discovered another rooftop sheep, though this one –

Ivelet Bridge

A Swaledale
resident

lodged atop the Bridge Inn – also balances an electric guitar on its
snout. The pub doesn't really need to attract attention to itself in this
way – it's a warm, friendly inn offering sensibly priced food and bed
and breakfast accommodation.

This had proved to be quite a wet day – with rain on the outside
and tea galore on the inside. Whatever the weather, Swaledale is such
a welcoming dale, despite its rugged beauty, that your recollections of
it will be infused with the kind of warm inner glow associated with a
newly mashed pot of Yorkshire tea.

Fact File

A Day in a Dale

Farmers Arms
Muker, Richmond DL11 6QG
☎ 01748 886 297
www.farmersarmsmuker.co.uk

Bridge House
Bed and Breakfast, Muker,
Richmond DL11 6QG
☎ 01748 886461
www.bridgehousemuker.co.uk

Punch Bowl Inn
Low Row, Richmond, N Yorkshire
☎ 01748 886 233
www.pbinn.co.uk

Bridge Inn
Grinton, Richmond,
North Yorkshire, DL11 6HH
☎ 01748 884224
www.bridgeinn-grinton.co.uk

Ghyllfoot Tearoom
Gunnerside, North Yorkshire
DL11 6LA
☎ 01748 886239

The White House Tearoom
Reeth, Richmond, North Yorkshire
☎ 01748 884763

A field
barn near
Keld

THE SECLUDED DALE
West Stonesdale (March)

Keld, as mentioned previously, is a small, tight-knit community of stone-built cottages, chapels, holiday homes and a campsite in the northern-most part of Swaledale before the valley merges into Birk Dale. Walkers know the village well because it is a stopover point on the Coast to Coast walk and the Pennine Way, as well as featuring on James Herriot's Youth Hostel walk. The former Youth Hostel continues to thrive in its new incarnation as Keld Lodge, the pub, restaurant and hotel we first visited when exploring Birk Dale.

We arrived on a bright, sunny but bracing March day with the aim of heading a little upstream before aiming due north to explore West Stonesdale, a remote but accessible dale that leads to Britain's highest pub at Tan Hill. We parked at Park Lodge farm in Keld (where there is an honesty box) to explore the village and the banks of the Swale. A pleasant stroll through the campsite leads you towards Hoggarts Leap, a stepped cascade of fast-flowing water, but just one of many impressive falls hereabouts; immediately below the farm, for example, is the less accessible Catrake Force. On previous visits we have followed the Swale south to see the lovely East Gill falls and Kisdon Force but this time we chose to explore the village in a more detail – which is how we met Cyril Purver.

A Day In A Dale

Cyril and his wife Peggy are retired civil servants from Reading in Berkshire, and have lived for close to thirty years in Tutil House, part of a lovely terrace with superb views towards Tutil Hill, named after a Viking king. 'We started coming up here in the 1970s when we were working in London,' says Cyril. 'I was talking to a colleague about where we might go on holiday and he suggested Swaledale. I said, "Where is that?" At that time it was even more rural than it is now – the bank used to come here every week with a till.'

Cyril and Peggy were great walkers, having explored all the local fells in their time. 'We are both over eighty now,' he explains, 'so we don't do as much walking as we used to but we've walked all these hills at one time or another. It's a wonderful place to live – even when we got two feet of snow this winter,' he chuckles. Cyril welcomes the recent opening of the Keld Lodge Hotel, as do the other twenty-three local inhabitants. 'All the villagers are very happy we have a pub again,' says Cyril. 'There used to be one here called the Catrake Inn which was bought by a strict Methodist farmer. Once he'd bought it, he promptly closed it down and renamed it Hope House, after the

West
Stonesdale

Band of Hope.' The popular Keld Lodge is unlikely to suffer a similar fate, hopefully.

A little uphill from Tutil House is the Keld United Reform Church, a modest but attractive chapel with the tiniest of bell towers, quaintly adjoining what is now a holiday cottage. The churchyard boasts one of the best views in the whole of Yorkshire. Not a bad place to moulder! Inside this simplest of churches are dark wooden pews set off by the whitewashed walls. Though the inscription outside says 'rebuilt in 1880' a historical display makes reference to a chapel in Keld as far back as 1510. There are four names on the 1914-18 war remembrance plaque including Robert Rukin – the surname of the present owners of Park Lodge farm.

Cyril advised us to seek out George Calvert, another villager, who has lived in Upper Swaledale for every one of his eighty-eight years (at the time of writing). We found him at Rose Cottage, next to the chapel, and he was happy to while away some time with us. 'I was born at Hoggarts Farm about two miles up the road,' he begins. 'I came to school here in Keld. There were thirty of us at the school but nearly everybody is gone now. There is one left who was best man at my wedding – Simon Fawcett – who was a gamekeeper. I still see him sometimes. From school I went to work on the farm – I farmed it all my life. I have two sons and they farm up there now.' George has been living at Rose Cottage for five years, having retired from farming some fifteen years ago.

George's family has been working the land locally for well over two hundred years. 'My grandfather came to it in eighteen-something. We are tenant farmers – the owners are really good landlords who live down in the south. We've generally kept between about five and six hundred sheep – there's a lot of common ground round here and it's good for keeping sheep, and good for grouse. We used to go beating from the twelfth of August. The land belonged to Lord Rochdale at Gunnerside Lodge at the time and he had three gamekeepers. We'd earn seven and sixpence a day working for three or four days: that was much more than you could earn as a farmer working all hours. When my father finished farming, my wife and I took the farm on and we had it for forty years.'

It's clear that George loved his life as a farmer, even if this highland region of Swaledale is one of the toughest places in the country to work the land. 'It's worth a lot to be your own boss,' says George. 'I didn't ever have to ask somebody what to do. You'd get up on a morning and think, 'We'll do some haymaking today or some wall repairing.' And if there was a show on we could have a day off without having to ask anybody.' George understands, if a little regretfully, that his way of life is gradually dying out. 'There's not so many people following farming now here as there once was. After the age of eleven, they go down to Richmond School where they see a different way of life. It's too lonely up here and too hard work. A lot of farms have amalgamated as well, so things have changed a bit. And now, when I go up to the farm and see how hard my sons and their wives are working, I feel as though I'm skiving!'

At the junction of the B6270 with Stonesdale Lane we found Park House campsite and Keld Bunkhouse, where we spoke briefly to the new owners, Steve and Heather Swann who have been there since May 2009. They cater mostly for walkers and campers, with a well-appointed and comfortable bunkhouse which overlooks its own sizeable waterfall, Rainby Force. The visitors' book contained only superlatives from a series of extremely happy, satisfied clients.

Once past the bunkhouse you turn right over Park Bridge with views upstream of the Swale towards Wain Wath Falls. Immediately you find yourself negotiating a gear-testing hairpin bend leading upwards and onwards into West Stonesdale proper. The hamlet of West Stonesdale is ruggedly charming and based around a farm that belongs to the Thornborrow family who have farmed here for generations. Beyond this tiny village you see the road snaking into the

Rose Cottage resident George Calvert was born at Hoggarts Farm

The Pennine
Way at Tan Hill

distance, leading you up and into a shallow bowl-like plateau that feels like the top of the world. Tumbledown sheep pens dot the landscape while innumerable becks straggle either side of the winding lane and narrow bridges. On the day of our visit, the paradoxically beautiful bleakness was emphasised by significant patches of March snow, remnants of one of the hardest winters in a generation. Perhaps the snow made it harder to spot the Swaledale sheep: the ones we did see were grazing close to the side of the road, or even on it.

Arriving at Tan Hill Inn, one thousand seven hundred and thirty-two feet above sea level, the horizon opens up before you: an alluring combination of stark isolation, rugged landscape and breathtaking views. We arrived by car but the recommended alternative is to land on the doorstep in muddy boots having walked the four and a half miles from Keld or the eight miles from Bowes by means of the Pennine Way, which opened in 1965. Ewe Juice is the local ale – only available here at the Tan Hill Inn, though brewed in Dentdale. The first recorded inn at Tan Hill was in 1586, with evidence of coal mining in the vicinity from the twelfth century. When the last mine closed in

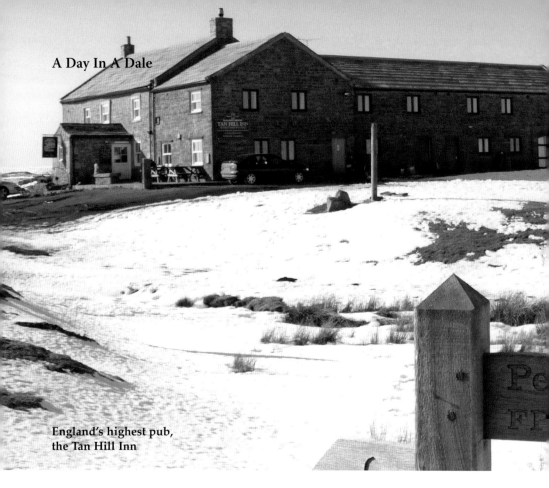

**England's highest pub,
the Tan Hill Inn**

1929 this hardy pub still kept going, supported by its even hardier clientele. In 1995 Tan Hill added to its fame (already guaranteed by its location and by double-glazing adverts on television) by becoming the first public house in England to get a licence for weddings.

In 2005 Alex and Mary Baines sold the inn to Mike Peace and Tracy Daly. Tracy put the property up for sale in 2008 for a price tag of just over a million pounds – but it still hadn't sold at the time of our visit. 2008 was also the year in which the Arctic Monkeys played here to an estimated audience in excess of fifteen hundred. At New Year 2009, the pub again hit the headlines when guests found themselves snowed in for several days. 'There were phone calls from newspapers, TV and radio stations from all over the world the day after everyone got out again,' says bar manager Sharon Saul. 'There's never a dull moment up here.'

So, however you choose to tackle West Stonesdale, you are at least guaranteed the comforts of a pub at either end of the journey and, if this forms part of an even longer walk, a bed for the night.

Fact File

Butt House (*bed and breakfast*),
Keld, North Yorkshire
☎ 01748 886374
⌂www.coasttocoastguides.co.uk

Park Lodge Camp Site
Keld, North Yorkshire DL11 6LJ
☎ 01748 886274
⌂www.rukins-keld.co.uk

Keld Lodge
Keld, North Yorkshire DL11 6LL
☎ 01748 886259
⌂www.keldlodge.com

Keld Bunkhouse
Park House, North Yorkshire
DL11 6DZ
☎ 01748 886549
⌂www.keldbunkhouse.com

The Tan Hill Inn
Reeth, North Yorkshire DL11 6ED
☎ 01833 628246
⌂www.tanhillinn.com

A view of
Arkengarthdale

THE OTHER FORGOTTEN DALE
Arkengarthdale (November)

Arkengarthdale is the most northerly of the Yorkshire dales and whose name is arguably the most evocative. On isolated stretches of its timeless moorland road that eventually leads into the bleakest of terrain (though worth driving through if you want to reach England's highest pub at Tan Hill), it would come as little surprise to encounter Arkil, the eleventh century Norse chieftain after whom the dale is reputedly named. You are more likely, though, to come across recalcitrant sheep who regard the road as their right of way, not yours.

In our exploration into this lesser known dale – indeed, Arkengarthdale has been referred to as 'The Forgotten Dale' – we were blessed by beautiful early November weather. We drove up through Wharfedale and Coverdale – the other 'forgotten' dale – to Middleham, on to Leyburn, and into Swaledale.

Heading west along the valley, you enter into Reeth's welcoming embrace, with its encircling collection of hotels, pubs, restaurants, tearooms, gift shops and ice cream parlour set around a network of lanes that criss-cross and sub-divide its sloping central green. What distinguishes this village green from almost any other is that from one of its corners you are twenty feet or so below its highest point.

Though our main aim was to venture a little further north in search of Arkengarthdale's capital, the village of Langthwaite, just to the north of which is the celebrated CB Inn, we felt obliged to linger a little longer in Reeth, the hub of Swaledale and entrance to the valley of the Arkle Beck. The village itself warmly surrounds you with its appealing range of enduring architecture, while the hills of Fremington Edge to the east, Calver Hill to the north and west, and Harkerside Moor to the south of the Swale provide a reassuring and protectively enclosing horizon.

At the centre of the green, a sizeable pile of combustible material had been gathered in preparation for Bonfire Night, a metaphorical (though ultimately literal) indication of the warmth of community endeavour. The impression gained is that Reeth is a place of artists and artisans (the French potter Monica Young lived and worked here until her death in 2004, coming to Reeth via Paris, Barcelona and Madrid), of people who work the land, traders, and those who gladly welcome tourists all year long. It's very much a living village, as testified to in part by its thriving post office and grocery store.

Certain features stand out: its row of pubs, including The Black Bull (which, quirkily, has one of its signs upside down), The Kings Arms and The Buck; the 1868 water pump; the elegant Burgoyne

Langthwaite

Powder House

Country House hotel and restaurant; the war memorial; and the distinctively-shaped Methodist church on the opposite side of the green.

One of the hidden gems of Reeth, nestling in a back street, is the local museum. It is a lovely, antiquated place run, with obvious affection and attention to detail, by Helen Bainbridge and her husband Alan. Walking around the museum induces the kind of cosy feeling of being in your grandmother's attic and discovering lots of interesting bits and pieces from the past. There are family photographs, various household and domestic appliances that make you feel old when you realise there was one just like it in your house as a child, and displays about the history of the area. There is an informative section, for example, about the lead mining industry, which was rife all over the Yorkshire Dales for the period between 1830 and 1890, during which time Arkengarthdale was the most productive vein.

A Day In A Dale

The bridge at
Bleaberry Gill

Helen also told us about the history of the building itself which was built as a Methodist school in 1836. During the Second World War it became a billeting station for soldiers doing their six week battle training at Catterick Camp, housing up to thirty men at a time. Then, after the war, the building was used as a place for putting on entertainments for the local people, including an annual pantomime. 'This year we are putting on the panto, *Beauty and the Beast*, which was originally performed here in January 1949,' says Helen. 'I found one of the old scripts and someone suggested that we put the panto on. I never thought we'd actually do it, but the response from the people in the village has been amazing.'

Reeth, at the very southern tip of Arkengarthdale's ten-mile length, is the ideal base to explore 'The Forgotten Dale'. There are plenty of places to stay and out of season it is especially peaceful: once you head north, you are instantly in a quieter world and able to enjoy the quite staggering beauty of the surrounding landscape, the perfect antidote to today's hectic lifestyle. At the height of the lead-mining industry the dale had a population of over fifteen hundred: today, fewer than two hundred people live here.

A Day In A Dale

The village of Langthwaite, which is the only sizeable settlement in the whole of Arkengarthdale, is probably best known these days for the fact that its attractive stone bridge over Arkle Beck was used in the opening credits of the popular BBC TV series based on James Herriot's books, *All Creatures Great and Small*.

It really is a charming, if tiny, village, its narrow, winding lanes and stone buildings unchanged for two centuries and therefore ideal as a period location, as well as a beautiful place to live. We stopped for a quick bite to eat at The Red Lion, an appealingly old-fashioned establishment – a comfortable combination of pub, village shop and someone's front room. Simple fare was on offer and we had a tasty pastie, nice and hot, which kept out the chill on a clear but crisp autumnal day. We met a retired couple who live in Darlington but choose to drive twice a week to visit the pub.

If you fancy something a tad more sophisticated, then the C B Inn is the place to go. In a commanding position on the moor top, this eighteenth century coaching inn is a most convivial place to spend some time – and no doubt would have been a welcoming sight in days gone by for coach travellers traversing this remote part of the world on a bleak night.

The inn's initials stand for Charles Bathurst, an eighteenth century

St Mary's - a 'Waterloo' church

Arkengarthdale

entrepreneur and lead-mine owner. It's another Charles, Charles Cody, who, with his wife Stacy, can now offer guests a choice from nineteen en-suite rooms and a superb range of high-quality meals. The roaring fire was an especially welcome feature to greet us on the day of our visit – blue as the skies were, the temperature outside was dropping fast. Anyone beforehand who had heard of our intention to visit Arkengathdale immediately responded by saying, 'Ah, yes – the C B Inn!' And now we know why. With its stripped pine, spacious public rooms (with alcoves here and there), it's a remarkable oasis of an inn, and far larger on the inside than you might imagine from a cursory external view.

From the back terrace, there are superb views south down the valley, and east towards the impressive Scar House. The friendly barmaid informed us this was a hunting lodge, the property of The Duke of Norfolk. Certainly, the local moors are known for their grouse. With the late autumns we now get, the variety of colours in the foliage of the trees surrounding Scar House made it a view to savour.

Just to the north of the inn is an intriguing collection of houses on a triangular plot and known as the C B Yard. This was once the administrative centre for lead-mining in the dale. The buildings previously housed workshops for joiners and blacksmiths, a peat store, a saw mill and offices and lodging for the agent of the mine owners. The Yard is now private housing. In an adjoining field you see

Bleaberry Gill

the even more intriguing Powder House, a delightful hexagonal edifice sited well away from other buildings since the powder that would have been housed here was, of course, gunpowder. There was no sign of a bonfire being built in this field!

Between the two taverns is St Mary's church, built on a budget in 1820 but an enduring legacy to the craft and skill of its constructors. St Mary's was one of the six hundred so-called 'Waterloo' churches constructed in the period after Napoleon's defeat both for celebratory purposes but also to help bolster Conformist church-going at a time when the Church's authority was being challenged. Evidence of the limited funding available is that the church boasts no stained glass, but it is a decidedly imposing man-made object within one of the loveliest spot's in God's Own Country.

Arkengarthdale has a number of tiny hamlets whose names all betray the influence of Norse invaders: Whaw (reached by a beautiful arched bridge); Booze – which sadly has no pub, but you have to pass The Red Lion to get there; Arkle Town, with its little collection of pre-war petrol pumps standing in a redundant line in their own lay-by; Eskeleth; Raw: all hamlets founded by the princes of the Danes.

Just south of the C B Inn is a turning west towards Low Row. If you have time, you should drive the length of this narrow, winding road to discover the famous water splash or ford across Bleaberry Gill which is also featured in the opening credits of *All Creatures Great and Small*.

There's a little white-painted foot-bridge here now in a spot where it's impossible not to stop and feel as if you have been transported back in time. In the hollow of this enchanting place, you cannot see any sign of habitation. It's somewhere to let your mind drift off in peaceful reverie – or to bring the kids for a picnic.

We drove home through the rest of sumptuous Swaledale – a journey which, as the constantly changing late autumn light enhanced the rich colours of the breathtaking landscape, confirmed our view that the delights of the dales are never-ending.

Fact File

The Swaledale Museum
Reeth, North Yorkshire DL11 6QT
☎ 01748 884118
www.swaledalemuseum.org
Accommodation is also available in the Museum Cottage.

The CB Inn
Arkengarthdale, Richmond,
North Yorkshire DL11 6EN
☎ 01748 884567
www.cbinn.co.uk

The Red Lion
Langthwaite, North Yorkshire
DL11 6RE
☎ 01748 884218
www.redlionlangthwaite.co.uk

The Black Bull
High Row, Reeth,
North Yorkshire DL11 6SZ
☎ 01748 884213
www.theblackbullreeth.co.uk

The Kings Arms Hotel
Reeth, North Yorkshire DL11 6SY
☎ 01748 884259
www.thekingsarms.com

The Buck Hotel
Reeth, North Yorkshire DL11 6SW
☎ 01748 884210
www.buckhotel.co.uk

The White House tearoom
Reeth
☎ 01748 884763

The Yorkshire Dales National Park Information centre at Reeth sells maps and leaflets on walks in the area.
☎ 01748 884059.

Burgoyne House Hotel and Restaurant
Reeth, North Yorkshire DL11 6SN
☎ 01748 884292
www.theburgoyne.co.uk

ADDENDUM

Lothersdale, Upper Nidderdale, Barbondale

There are three further dales that we chose to visit as part of this series, none of which is located in the Yorkshire Dales National Park. However, we consider them to be of equal interest to all the other dales we have explored for the purposes of this book. Lothersdale lies further to the south of what are sometimes called the Southern Dales, and borders Pendle Hill and Lancashire. Nidderdale is the most easterly of the dales we have visited but is surprisingly close to both Coverdale and Wensleydale, as well as being a designated Area of Outstanding Natural Beauty. Barbondale currently lies outside of the National Park and beyond the Yorkshire border, to the south of Dent, accessed via a road that eventually leads to the A65 and Kirkby Lonsdale: there are interesting rumours, however, suggesting that Barbondale may well soon be incorporated into the National Park with all its attendant benefits. We did not feel that any of these three dales should be neglected, especially given their proximity to all of the beautiful 'official' dales that it has been our pleasure to discover more fully.

A lane in
Lothersdale

THE DIVINE DALE
Lothersdale (June)

Lothersdale is not so much a dale as a lovely village with a beck running through it. Inevitably, the surrounding area has acquired the village's name, making it one of the smallest of the lesser-sized dales in Yorkshire. Though not far from the main road running between Crosshills and Colne, once you divert onto the country lanes you are instantly transported into a bygone age where it's hard for two cars to pass each other and signposts are misleading or non-existent.

What distinguishes the upland areas around Lothersdale are the various vistas, with far-reaching views east along the Airedale valley, north-east towards Beamsley Beacon and west towards Lancashire and Pendle Hill. Each new lane you dip down into and then ascend offers you a different, engaging perspective.

We started our journey by heading westwards out of Crosshills, then turning right onto Carr Head Lane at Malsis Independent School (boarding and day pupils). The main building epitomises the kind of fictional boarding schools from children's literature that hold such appeal for young readers. Further along this minor road, we stopped to admire the rhododendrons in the driveway for Carr Head Hall before turning off on the loop which eventually brings you to Over House Farm.

From this extremely narrow lane we gained a view across to Stone Gappe in the distance, the house just outside the village of Lothersdale where Charlotte Bronte worked briefly as a governess in 1839. It's a house that she was to immortalise in Jane Eyre – but more of that later.

The view eastwards from just past the farm and along the lane is particularly beautiful. It's here, also, that the two hundred and seventy mile long Pennine Way passes through the landscape on its route north towards the village before branching north-westwards in the direction of Thornton-in-Craven, and then north again towards Malham.

At this point on the journey towards Lothersdale village you can't help feeling you are exploring a kind of secret dale with various windows onto enchanting horizons. Everywhere you look there seem to be little lanes criss-crossing the landscape, punctuated by occasional neatly-kept farmyards and buildings. Nowhere in the region rises much over three hundred and fifty metres above sea level, but many of the hills catch your eye because of their distinctive and unusual contours.

We briefly made a little detour out of Yorkshire and into the Pendle district. This was unintentional – it was the lack of signposts again – but it was worth it, firstly because we discovered that the road had the wonderful name of Warley Wise Lane and, secondly, we found the intriguingly named Black Lane Ends pub at the end of it. This looked inviting, is open all day for food and serves beer from the Skipton-based Copper Dragon brewery.

We made a break for the border by turning right, which is back towards the village. As we approached the houses, looking down into the steep-sided valley we saw a lady striding up the hill while walking three dogs. When we pulled over for a chat, Rona Duncan told us that she had been living in Lothersdale for thirteen years and that it was a lovely place to live. 'It took a while to get to know people, but it is very friendly. The scenery is fantastic although it does get a bit hairy in winter.' Originally from Edinburgh, she said that the hills around the village reminded her of the lowlands of Scotland. 'I'm certainly not homesick anymore.' Earlier we had spotted a quirky little hill and we enquired whether she knew the name of it. 'Oh, that's in Lancashire,' she jokingly replied, 'so we don't bother about that.' Looking on the map didn't provide any answers either, though it did reveal that nearby there was the eyebrow-raising feature known as Roger Moor. It's a steep gradient down into the village, with heather-covered banks on either side which must look magnificent in August. Once in Lothersdale itself, you should park the car, as we did, and explore on foot. The impression is of a busy, thriving village which has a primary school, a war memorial, club house, a cemetery and an old Methodist chapel (Bethel Chapel) dating back to 1851. On a terrace of charming little cottages called Rose-in-the-Dale was a plaque dedicated to Mary Hayes of Raygill (1893-1967), the daughter of William Spencer, 'through whose generosity Lothersdale is richly endowed.'

Nearby Raygill was quarried for lime as early as the seventeenth century and then mined for barytes, used in the oil and gas industries as well as an ingredient of barium meals. For a while in the mid-nineteenth century Raygill became the largest producer of barytes in the country. The discovery in 1875 of pre-historic animal remains in the quarry led to further excavations which revealed the Raygill Fissure. It contained the fossilised bones of creatures you are unlikely to see running wild anywhere in Yorkshire today: elephant, rhinoceros, roebuck, hyena, lion, hippopotamus and bear. When the quarry closed in 1987 it was bought by Bernard Clement who landscaped the site and stocked four man-made lakes with a variety of fish. Anglers travel here from all over the country to cast their lines in a peaceful and picturesque setting.

At the bottom end of Lothersdale village is The Hare and Hounds pub which unfortunately wasn't open at the time of our visit. Christ Church, C of E church, constructed in 1838, lies further up the hill heading east. This was the church that Charlotte Bronte attended while she was working at Stone Gappe the following year – her employer, Mr John Benson Sidgwick, was instrumental in the church's founding.

The church itself is quite austere, both externally and internally. Presumably this lack of decoration or ornamentation was due to the Methodist influence in the area. However, there are three attractive stained glass windows and a memorial to the men of the village who perished in the two World Wars. A separate memorial tablet is dedicated to one unfortunate young man: though only nineteen at the time of his death, Autbert Christopher Cedric Dutton of the 3rd South

African Infantry had 'fought against the Senussi in Egypt', was wounded in the Battle of the Somme in 1916 and finally perished at Ypres in September 1917.

In the church porch we found an informative book compiled by local people to celebrate the Millennium. A quick leaf through provided an impression of a contented, tight-knit community of people who feel a great deal of pride and affection for their village. Though Lothersdale is made up of only around two hundred dwellings, there is plenty going on – the Young Farmers, the Women's Institute, and the Mothers' Union are all groups with strong memberships, while the Lothersdale Singers perform regularly in the village and surrounding area.

The Spencer family, long established in the village for generations, and certainly around when Charlotte Bronte had her brief sojourn there, are mentioned in the Millennium book as providing the village

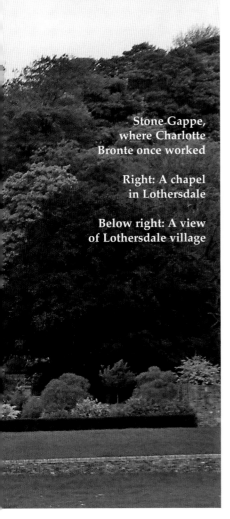

Stone Gappe, where Charlotte Bronte once worked

Right: A chapel in Lothersdale

Below right: A view of Lothersdale village

with many facilities. William Spencer who, according to a plaque in the church, was church warden for an impressive sixty-eight years, set up the Lothersdale Village Trust in 1928. Its purpose is to support the recreational activities of the community. A house, now the Village Clubhouse, was left to be managed by the trust. It charges rental fees to support various local clubs and events.

The population of the village has remained fairly constant and, although there are no longer any working farms within the village proper, we saw plenty of evidence that the farming tradition still continues nearby. The Primary School almost closed in the 1980s but is now flourishing; the Post Office, however, is now closed but managed to keep going until 1998. The book ends with a quotation that best sums up the spirit of the village: Mr Kenneth Wilson said, in 1958, 'We have a wonderful life in Lothersdale. Such a happy going on between everybody.'

227

The Leeds-Liverpool canal near Cononley

Leaving the village, we stopped just beyond Stone Gappe. This literary landmark (now owned by McAlpine's) is no longer accessible to the public though it features in many guides to the Brontes as the inspiration for Gateshead Hall, home of the Reed family in the opening chapters of *Jane Eyre*. Intriguingly, the neighbouring house to Stone Gappe is called Gates Head. Charlotte Bronte's relatively unhappy spell here as a governess looking after the Sidgwicks' spoilt, 'riotous' children (one threw a bible at her) clearly suggested material for how Jane was bullied in her younger years by her unlovely cousins. Nevertheless, Charlotte found the surrounding countryside 'divine', as expressed in a letter to her sister Emily. There is a public footpath below the property leading to a new private driveway: however, it's difficult to see much of the house itself due to a retaining garden wall that has been built by the current owners. What you can enjoy today, though, is the same view down into the valley that Charlotte was so enchanted by.

As we headed away from Lothersdale village, we got a glimpse of an old chimney on the horizon with what may have been a disused lime quarry in the foreground. We would have been interested to explore further but for the private property sign on the entrance to the track that led up to it. Further along, a right turn took us down to the village of Cononley (no signpost again) and we slowly descended a very steep hill. On a bend in the road was a well-placed bench, ideal for admiring the magnificent views or for just having a breather, with the inscription 'rest and be thankful'.

Entering the village, you come into 'Main Street' which, despite its name, begins as a tiny, narrow road with pretty stone cottages on either side such as you might expect to find in the middle of the Dorset countryside (or even Brittany). The road then opens out as you drive past the grand-looking Cononley Hall, now a bed and breakfast establishment. An old stone bridge arches over a small beck which flows towards the nearby River Aire. Cononley, unlike Lothersdale, has a post office and village shop but also the modern trappings of a Chinese takeaway and a commuter-friendly railway station.

Having waited at the level crossing for a Bradford train to go past, we drove across and very quickly found ourselves back on the busy A629 – and a thousand miles away from the rural tranquillity of the 'divine' dale.

Fact File

Raygill Fisheries
1 Raygill Cottage, Lothersdale,
Skipton, North Yorkshire BD20 8HH
☎ 01535 632500
⌂ www.raygillfisheries.co.uk

Cononley Hall
Georgian House Bed and Breakfast,
Main Street, Cononley BD20 8LJ
☎ 01535 633923
⌂ www.cononleyhall.co.uk

Black Lane Ends pub
near Colne,
on the Skipton Old Road BB8 7EP
☎ 01282 863070

The Hare and Hounds
Lothersdale, Keighley,
West Yorkshire BD20 8EL
☎ 01535 630977

How Stean Gorge
in Niddersdale

THE WELCOMING DALE
Upper Nidderdale (November)

There are many approaches to Pateley Bridge, the starting point for a journey into Upper Nidderdale. The network of country lanes and minor roads between here and Otley alone would have kept a cartload of cartographers happy for weeks on end. Perhaps the most dramatic route is from the direction of Grassington and Greenhow which entails a winding descent into the town, while at the same time providing superb views over much of Nidderdale, views which explain why this dale has been designated an Area of Outstanding Natural Beauty.

A brief detour via Bewerley (for the town should properly be known as Pateley Bridge with Bewerley) permits the opportunity to visit the nearby local landmark known as the Two Stoopes. These distinctive structures on a hill just outside Pateley Bridge were erected around 1810 by labourers working for John Yorke of Bewerley Hall. In a touching act of philanthropy, Yorke commissioned the folly when work was scarce in order to keep his labourers in employment and above the poverty line. Each labourer was paid a shilling a day and a loaf of bread. There were originally three pillars – presumably resembling a giant set of cricket stumps – and the folly was known locally as the Three Stoopes until a violent storm in November 1893 when one of the pillars was blown down. The views from here both over Pateley Bridge and into the distance are simply stunning; it's small wonder that the place is so popular with local and visiting walkers alike.

Pateley Bridge itself is a welcoming town with a relaxed yet sophisticated feel to it reflected in the number of inviting cafes, restaurants, delis and wine merchants that line the steep, narrow high street along with a couple of handsome Georgian coaching inns, award-winning butchers, a baker's, florist and an art gallery. Local resident and Parish Councillor Quentin Sands, who has lived in Pateley Bridge for ten years, explains the town's allure: 'It is an unpretentious working town with a good mix of people. There are opportunities for fine living – plenty of good restaurants and a great annual arts festival – added to which you have beautiful natural wonders on your doorstep.'

One of the shops on the high street is the Oldest Sweet Shop in England. A family-run business established in 1827, it is housed in a building that dates back to the 1630s. Run by Keith and Gloria Tordoff, their son Alex and his partner Kirsty Shepherd, it is a cosy emporium for the sweet-toothed, full of evocative sugar-and-spice aromas. Robbie Coltrane visited during the filming of his ITV series, *B-Road Britain*. 'He was a really nice guy,' says Kirsty. 'People heard about his visit, so the place was very busy.' The week after the programme was broadcast the shop was overrun. 'People queued for up to two hours outside,' says Kirsty. 'They had come from all over the country. There was a family from Devon and another from Aberdeen. There was even a couple who had flown over from Spain specially!'

The programme obviously boosted the shop's business immediately after it was shown, but there is no shortage of trade even without extra publicity. 'We have locals who are regular customers,' says Alex 'and we also get a lot a tourists coming in all year round.' The Tordoffs will track down particular sweets for customers, if they can, through their extensive contacts in the confectionery world and, to prove that they really are old-fashioned, the original Victorian till they still use in the shop only accepts cash or cheques.

The Apothecary's House is another lovely old building on the high street which dates back four hundred years and is now an attractive tea room run by Yoshi and Jon Levy. By day it is a traditional English tea

INSET: Stan Beer, proprietor of How Stean Gorge

The view across Nidderdale from the Two Stoopes

room serving light lunches and home baked cakes and scones; by night it becomes a Japanese restaurant. They formerly ran a restaurant in Oxford, but have settled very happily in Pateley Bridge. 'We had been coming up here on holiday for a few years and we really liked it,' says Yoshi who is originally from Hiroshima. 'Then, when our son was born two years ago, we decided to move somewhere more rural.' They started looking for a place where they could run a restaurant and live above it – and, since they liked Pateley Bridge so much, they came to

Pateley Bridge

see what was on offer. As soon as they walked into the Apothecary's House Yoshi knew they had found their new home. 'It reminded me of my grandparents' house in Japan,' she says with a fond smile. 'It has such a lovely feeling about it and is so full of history.' In fact, some of the beams on the ceiling were once part of one of Henry VIII's warships.

A short, uphill walk out of Pateley Bridge will bring you to the ancient church of St Mary the Virgin, a wonderfully atmospheric place. The lichen-covered ruin of the church is surrounded by elegantly worn and weathered gravestones, each of which tells a story – sometimes poignant, sometimes mysterious, and occasionally surprising, as in the case of Mary Myers who died in 1743 'aged near one hundred and twenty years'.

West of the town's bridge is a turning to the right leading you into Upper Nidderdale. Passing the Bridge Inn you soon arrive at Gouthwaite Reservoir, one of three such man-made lakes which are fed by the River Nidd and which dominate this portion of the dale. At the northern tip of Gouthwaite lies the small, enchanting hamlet of

Ramsgill which boasts the Yorke Arms Hotel, famed nationally for the quality of its cuisine.

It's worth saying at this point that Nidderdale has its own circular (though it's rather a squashed circle) walk, some fifty three miles of designated and well signposted paths that lasso the upper regions of the Nidd. Abandoning your car and exploring on foot is highly recommended, especially as you can easily organise shorter or longer excursions to suit the time available and your energy levels. Both the eastern and western flanks of Gouthwaite reservoir, for example, form part of the Nidderdale Way – so to start and end at Ramsgill would make a splendid afternoon's outing.

Next stop for us was How Stean Gorge, a location where the River Nidd attempts a more than passable imitation of being a mountainous Swiss rivulet. A site of special scientific interest (SSSI), this is a wonderful place for a family day out. The spectacular wooded limestone gorge first opened to the public in 1869 and readily appealed to the Victorian affection for grottos and caves. Narrow footpaths and bridges cross the steep-sided ravine which is twenty metres deep at some points. It is a magical place to stroll around and is a short enough walk for even quite young children to enjoy – plus there is the added excitement of caves to explore, the biggest of which is Tom Taylor's cave. Legend has it that Tom was a notorious local highwayman who would hide his booty here. He came to a sticky end eventually when his hideout was discovered by the local constabulary.

The gorge is privately run by Stan Beer and his wife Ann who have been in situ since June 2007. 'I was a paramedic with the ambulance service,' says Stan who we caught up with when he was dangling precariously over a precipice (though secured by ropes) whilst engaged in a form of extreme gardening. 'We knew the previous owner, Howard Stevenson,' he explains. 'I used to do some bits and pieces of tree work for him and my daughter worked here in the café. When we heard that Howard was retiring we thought it would be a nice thing to do – so here we are. My wife, who is a retired nurse, is in charge of the kitchen and my daughter is waitressing: it's turned into a proper family business,' he smiles.

The café, which originally opened in 1902, offers good, home-cooked traditional food at reasonable prices – and is also open in the evenings. 'We have an alcohol licence now, so we are trying out new things,' says Stan. 'We are going to put on films and we are having a French evening with an accordion player.' There are also bikes for hire and Stan offers a service whereby he will drive people up to Scar House Reservoir with the bikes in the back of his van and then it's a relatively easy downhill ride back down to the gorge.

On a fine day Middlesmoor, a little further up from the gorge, is a paradise village. There are few communities anywhere else in England living quite so high above sea level and the panoramic views from here are commanding. By turning your gaze inwards, the local pub, the Crown Hotel, and the church, St Chad's, are delightful, as are the flower-bedecked cottages arrayed haphazardly above and to the sides of the church. However, at this altitude, the village must feel quite exposed in high winds or in the depths of winter.

Walkers can head north-west out of Middlesmoor on the Nidderdale Way to reach Scar House Reservoir on what is known as In Moor Lane. Drivers are obliged to head south-eastwards to Lofthouse (pronounced 'Loftus'), locate the cricket club (with a tiny pitch that makes scant allowance for a bowler's run-up) and take the adjacent narrow lane (past the Fire Station) provided by Yorkshire Water as an access route to Scar House. The lane borders the river all the way to the reservoir and shows Nidderdale off at its best, particularly under blue skies and with the colours of autumn illuminating the trees with the richest imaginable reds and oranges and yellows.

Angram
Reservoir

Surrounded by a rugged landscape, the reservoir is a wild, windswept place, affording spectacular views. A stone monument honours the itinerant workers who built the reservoirs and other large works of engineering around the country, while an informative board details the history of the reservoir and its construction. Try to get a closer look at the impressively crenulated structure of the dam – which is almost six hundred metres long and rises to fifty five metres above the water. One can almost imagine the Grand Opening in 1936 as invited gentry, dressed in their finery, came to gaze with pride upon another wonder of the modern age.

Scar House was the last reservoir to be built in the Nidd Valley and it took fifteen years to complete. During its construction, a village was built just below the dam to house the workforce. Home to one thousand two hundred and fifty workers, its facilities included shops, a church, a concert hall, a cinema and a small hospital.

The short circular walk around the reservoir is thoroughly recommended, or, with enough Weetabix for breakfast, you might include the loop around Angram Reservoir to the south-west. Here you will find Great Whernside looming over you to the west, accompanied by the odd realisation that you are far closer to Kettlewell (as the crow flies) than you are to Pateley Bridge – with Bewerley.

Fact File

The Oldest Sweet Shop in Britain
39 High Street, Pateley Bridge
☎ 01423 712371
www.oldestsweetshop.co.uk

The Apothecary's House
37 High Street, Pateley Bridge, North Yorkshire HG3 5JZ.
☎ 01423 711767

The Crown Hotel
Middlesmoor, Harrogate North Yorkshire HG3 5ST
☎ 01423 755204
www.nidderdale.co.uk/crownhotel

How Stean Gorge
Lofthouse, Harrogate,
North Yorkshire HG3 5SF
☎ 01423 755666
www.howstean.co.uk

The Yorke Arms Hotel
Ramsgill, North Yorkshire HG3 5RL
☎ 01423 755243
www.yorke-arms.co.uk

The road
through
Barbondale

THE SUNLIGHT DALE
Barbondale (January)

Driving along the A65 on a cold January day can still be inspiring. Glimpses of the snow-capped Three Peaks as the sun broke through were obvious pleasures as were remarkable panoramas of the distant Lake District hills and mountains. Also tipped with gleaming snow, they seemed remarkably close thanks to the unusual quality of the morning light.

Having left Yorkshire we entered the village of Cowan Bridge which many will know as the location of the boarding school where four of the five Bronte sisters were educated, though in unfortunate circumstances. A plaque on the side of a building on the main road as you leave the village informs you that Maria, Elizabeth, Charlotte and Emily Bronte (Anne was too young to attend) boarded at the school between 1824 and 1825: what the plaque doesn't tell you was that the older sisters, Maria and Elizabeth, died as a consequence of illnesses contracted at the school and the two famous younger sisters – later the authors of *Jane Eyre* and *Wuthering Heights* respectively – were removed from the school by their father, Patrick, never to return.

Sadly, the Bronte girls were not the only children to die at this time either at the school or as a consequence of being pupils there though, as Juliet Barker points out in her biography of the family, boarding schools throughout the country in this period had poor records relating to sleeping arrangements, quality of food and clothing, and general welfare of children. The headmaster, the Reverend William Carus Wilson, was later represented by Charlotte in the unflattering portrait of Mr Brocklehurst of Lowood School in the early chapters of *Jane Eyre* and the association was later emphasised by Mrs Gaskell in her book *The Life of Charlotte Bronte* which almost led to a libel case. The school moved from Cowan Bridge to nearby Casterton in 1832 (though the plaque says 1833) since when it has flourished and is now one of the most highly regarded girls' boarding schools in the country.

Turning right off the A65 at Devils's Bridge, near Kirkby Lonsdale, you take the A683 in the direction of Sedburgh. Before long you come to Casterton, a village most of whose buildings form a part of the school. Definitely not an annexe to the school is the Pheasant Inn, an attractive eighteenth century whitewashed building that, unfortunately, on the day of our visit wasn't open for business at lunchtime.

Instead we visited the nearby church, Holy Trinity, located on a bend in the main road near the entrance to the school. The church's enchanting interior – which features a memorial tablet to William Carus Wilson – is enhanced by impressive wall paintings and stained glass windows by James Clarke R.A. (1858-1943) and the better known Henry Holiday (1839-1927), a close friend of Lewis Carroll, whose work in stained glass can be seen at Westminster Abbey.

Our next stop was the village of Barbon, accessed by turning right off the main road into Barbondale. At the war memorial, we turned right then parked up immediately at the Barbon Inn. As soon as we walked through the door we felt assured of a warm welcome, partly because of the log-burning range, partly because of the gentle black Labrador, Tess, the pub dog, and partly because of the hospitality of friendly New Zealand barmaid Yvonne Thorsen, who has been living around these parts for four years. 'We moved here because my husband came to play rugby for Kirkby Lonsdale,' she says. 'It's a lovely place to live.'

Though the bar area is cosily small, the rest of the inn offers dining for nearly forty customers – and upstairs there are ten bedrooms for guests. The history of the inn goes back to the seventeenth century with

A Barbondale sheepfold

a pew-like bench seat in the restaurant area dating back to the 1680s. The building is owned by Baron Shuttleworth, who also owns nearby Barbon Manor, built in 1862 by Sir James Kay-Shuttleworth, a friend and benefactor of Charlotte Bronte.

After having enjoyed an excellent lunch sitting by the fire, we met Sandra Grainger who, along with her sister, Joyce Mason, has been managing the historic pub, hotel and restaurant since 2006. Sandra has thirty years' experience as an hotelier – she also runs a bed and breakfast in Blackpool – but has a special affinity for Barbon Inn which, growing up in nearby Sedbergh, she has known since her childhood.

'In fact, my mum came to work here seventy years ago when she was fourteen,' says Sandra. 'She and her older sister were live-in chambermaids. They did cleaning and helping out in the kitchen, but they weren't allowed to be seen by the guests.' The sisters shared a room at the top of the house and were occasionally allowed to go to the local dance. 'My mum met my dad at a dance in the village hall here; he was from a local farming family.'

Situated close to the Yorkshire Dales and within easy reach of the Lake District, the inn is an ideal base for walkers and other holidaymakers while Sandra can also offer specially tailored golfing, cycling, horse-riding and fishing packages. 'We are quite busy year round,' she says. 'And we have lots of returning clients including some from Germany and Belgium. We are very well supported locally, too. We have quiz nights on the first Sunday of every month and on the second of January we had about twelve teams squeezed in here!' Sandra's sister Joyce and her husband were farmers but after the last Foot and Mouth crisis they decided to retire which is when Sandra persuaded her sister to go into partnership with her. 'We both love it here,' she says. 'We've known the place all our lives.'

Bright winter sunlight illuminated the village as we emerged from the warmth of the pub, the nearby tower of the church gleaming golden against the backdrop of a brilliantly blue sky. There's evidence of a church building on this site dating back to the time of Shakespeare. A church was built in 1815 but replaced some eighty years later in a design by Lancaster-based architects Henry Paley and Hubert Austin, a family firm renowned in the area throughout the Victorian era and into the twentieth century. Lady Shuttleworth laid the foundation stone in 1892, as well as donating a stained glass window, but it was not until 1898 that the new church, with its ornate lychgate, was completed. Look out for the sundial in the churchyard and the little statue of St Bartholomew set in an alcove above the unusual mesh door of the porch.

Barbondale
cast in shadow

The Kay-Shuttleworths now rent out the manor house, built in 1862, but, for some time now, the Barbon Manor Hillclimb, organised by the Westmorland Motor Club, has taken place on the driveway to the house on a steep meandering ascent. The record for the 890 yard course, from a standing start, is a remarkable 20.5 seconds. The event, which attracts many visitors, takes place three times a year.

You leave the village with quite a hill climb of your own if you are driving towards Gawthrop and Dent, where Barbondale creates a T-junction with Dentdale. Close to the village, the beck is known as Barbon Beck but for much of the five mile stretch of dale it is known as Barkin Beck, Barkin being the name of the ridge near Calf Top which, at six hundred and nine metres, is the highest point on the western side of the dale. Barbon High Fell, looking towards Crag Hill and Whernside, is on your right as you head roughly north-eastwards up the dale with the sun shining straight up the valley in the late afternoon. Whernside was snow-capped and, elsewhere, snow had survived the thaw if it lay at the foot of a dry stone wall or in a shaded cleft of hill. Glistening in the sun Whernside's peak, still dusted in white, was a quite magical sight.

Having driven the length of the dale, we turned around after a brief tour of Gawthrop (in Dentdale) and retraced our steps. Driving into the sun was not exactly fun but it did enable us to enjoy again the various features of Barbondale: the minor waterfalls, the extensive vistas, curious sheepfolds – like the one by the roadside designed by artist Andy Goldsworthy whose work features at the Yorkshire Sculpture Park – and dry stone walls that run in a straight line directly up the steepest of slopes.

The area to the east of Barbondale is characterised by pot holes, a popular spot being around Bullpot Farm close to Ease Gill and its extensive network of underground passages. We encountered a mini-bus full of schoolchildren from nearby Ingleborough Hall outdoor centre looking as if they had enjoyed a good day of exercise and activity on one of the sunnier days of this winter. Let's hope their experience was as unforgettable as our day had been and that they will want to keep on returning to this very special part of beautiful dales country.

Back in the village of Barbon, we popped into the local shop where

A snow-capped
Whernside

we met shopkeeper Peter Crook. Originally from Liverpool, he has been running the shop for the past seventeen years having moved to the village from Preston. 'I worked for Leyland Daf and when I was made redundant, along with around three thousand other people, I decided to make a go of my own business. It's hard work – ten hours a day, seven days a week – and you don't make a fortune, but we're happy; the countryside is really nice around here.' The shop also contains a post office – sadly, a rarity in many Dales villages these days – and stocks newspapers and all the essentials for local people. However, Peter, who is in his sixties, is planning to retire next year which leaves the future of the shop uncertain.

There are rumours that the Yorkshire Dales National Park wishes to include the whole of Barbondale within its boundaries, unsurprising given that it is one of the most self-contained and striking of the many dales we have visited. Barkin Beck has its origins within the National Park confines, and the whole valley forms a part of the significant geological feature known as the Dent Fault. Membership of the National Park brings certain obligations and restrictions (for example,

regarding planning consent) but the benefits for local businesses of the extra publicity that is generated make such membership very attractive. Whatever the future brings, the true measure of Barbondale's appeal is that it's worth leaving Yorkshire for, and well worth claiming as our own!

Fact File

A Day in a Dale

The Pheasant Inn
Casterton, Kirkby Lonsdale,
Cumbria LA6 2RX
☎ 015242 71230

🖰 www.pheasantinn.co.uk

Bullpot Farm
Casterton, Carnforth, Cumbria
LA6 2JP
Bunkhouse and camping facilities
☎ 015242 71837

🖰 www.campingbarns.net

The Barbon Inn & Restaurant
Barbon, Nr Kirkby Lonsdale,
Cumbria LA6 2LJ
☎ 015242 76233

🖰 www.barbon-inn.co.uk

Barbon Manor Hillclimb
- *details available through the
Westmorland Motor Club*
🖰 www.westmorlandmotorclub.co.uk

Yorkshire Dales National Park
🖰 www.yorkshiredales.org.uk

Index

Bolton Priory

Ingleborough

Old turnstile at
How Stean Gorge

The Yorke Arms
at Ramsgill

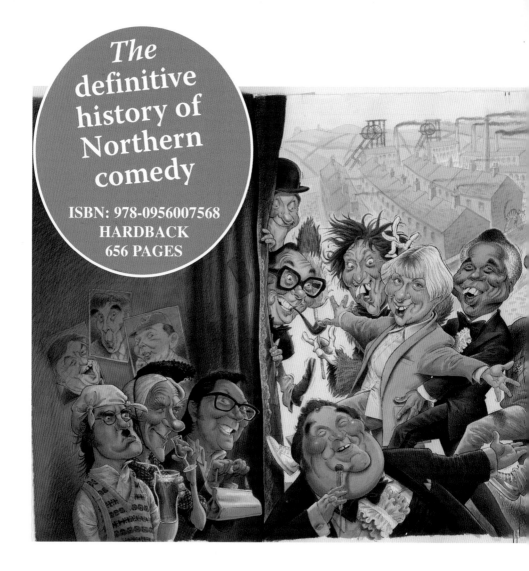

The
definitive
history of
Northern
comedy

ISBN: 978-0956007568
HARDBACK
656 PAGES

"...colourful & fascinating..."
- The Yorkshire Post

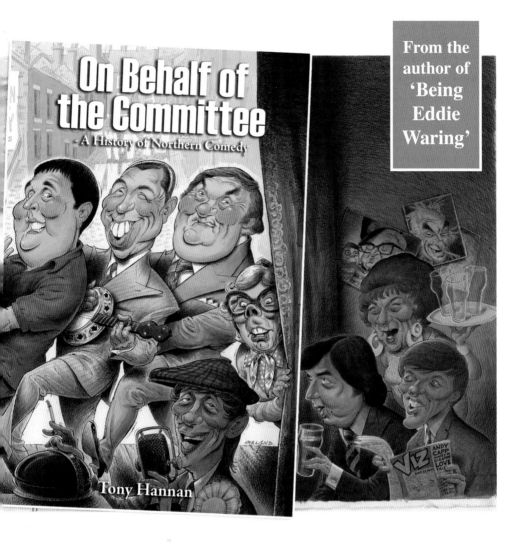

From the Industrial Revolution to our own comfortable 21st century digital age - via music hall, Variety, working mens clubs, radio, cinema & television - Northern-born comedians have consistently been at the heart of popular British comedy culture, tickling the funny bone of the entire nation.

This witty and informative book questions why that should be so, all the while charting an entertaining course through the careers of George Formby, Tommy Handley, Gracie Fields, Frank Randle, Al Read, Jimmy James, Hylda Baker, Jimmy Clitheroe, Les Dawson, Morecambe & Wise, Bernard Manning, Alan Bennett, Monty Python, Victoria Wood, Ken Dodd, Chubby Brown, The Young Ones, Vic and Bob, Steve Coogan, Caroline Aherne, the League of Gentlemen, Johnny Vegas, Peter Kay and many many others. Along the way, it also wonders why such a huge contribution to the British entertainment industry should be so often under-appreciated.

Mostly, however, it is a rich celebration of British comedy history & confirmation that you really do have to laugh - or else you'd cry...

COMING OCTOBER 2011
from Scratching Shed Publishing Ltd...

SWALEDALE SHEPHERDESS
Yvette Huddleston and Walter Swan

ISBN:978-0956478757

Scratching Shed Publishing Ltd